The Stringer

Written by
TED RALL

Art by
PABLO CALLEJO

NBM Graphic Novels
Nantier • Beall • Minoustchine
New York

ISBN 9781681122724

Library of Congress Control Number: 2020952003
Printed in Turkey
1st printing, April 2021

Also available wherever ebooks are sold, ISBN 9781681122731

Foreword

By Ted Rall

The news media is in trouble. Tens of thousands of journalists have been laid off in recent years, reducing newsroom employment to less than half of 20 years ago. During the same period, 2000 newspapers went out of business. So many local radio stations have closed or been absorbed by conglomerates that swaths of the nation have no way to find out that a tornado is headed their way.

The Internet offers searchable cross-referenced links to easily-accessible archives. As exciting as the new technology is, however, none of it means anything if the companies that pay to host that information go out of business and those vast stores of knowledge vanish into the cyber-ether.

What you might not know, what CEOs of media corporations don't even seem to know, is that this is not a new trend. Daily newspaper circulation peaked in 1984 at just over 63 million, at a time when the population of the United States was 236 million. In real terms, newspaper circulation has been declining since 1960. The year JFK beat Nixon, 59 million Americans picked up a daily paper—a figure that stayed roughly the same until the late 1980s. In 1960, however, there were only 181 million people. It's been all downhill since then. Radio and television killed a lot of newspaper circulation. The Internet was merely the last nail in the coffin.

Consumption of news media has radically changed over the last half century. As of 2018, one in five Americans said that they got their news from social media like Twitter and Facebook, more than the 16% who said they still read a daily newspaper. Yet production of the news has hardly changed. Experts estimate that 80% of the news you read on the Internet and watch on television originated in an old-fashioned dead-tree print newspaper. And those papers are dying.

And so is democracy. As Alexis de Tocqueville noted two centuries ago, the American democratic experiment could only succeed among a well-informed populace. The death of widely-accepted, reputable news organizations has opened a vacuum that has been filled by misinformation, disinformation, conspiracy theories, Internet scams, and fraud fueled by breathtakingly sophisticated technology. Local news reporting is critically endangered; this would be a great time to become a corrupt local or state politician. As a result we live in a dysfunctional society in which it is impossible to engage in political debate because it isn't just the opinions that are different depending on whether you are on the left or the right, facts that underlie the issues are themselves in dispute. We cannot agree on whether climate change is real or fiction, so how can we possibly debate solutions?

This is the cultural landscape that inspired "The Stringer." As I heard from one colleague after another tell me that he or she had been laid off, I wondered, how will they survive? Not everyone is married to someone who works in a growing industry like Silicon Valley. How would politics or business continue to be viable in an environment where facts were fungible? What would happen if victims of media disruption refused to go quietly into the good night?

Such a person might be much more dangerous than you might suppose.

That thought first crossed my mind over an overpriced beer in the early fall of 2010. I was hanging out at the Gandamack Lodge, a guest house in Kabul popular with journalists, NGO workers and "contractors"—a euphemism for mercenaries, assassins and other unsavory black-ops types—while trying to line up transportation across war-torn Afghanistan's "Central Highway"—a euphemism for a dirt track through jagged mountains. As I chatted with reporters for outlets from around the globe and watched the surreal scene as paid killers hooked up with professional do-gooders, I marveled at the wealth of information in the mind of even the most ordinary war correspondent.

They weren't all particularly educated or knowledgeable about the places they got parachuted in to cover. One correspondent for Al Jazeera shot up liquid courage in the form of locally-sourced heroin before donning a burqa and jumping into a taxi toward Taliban-controlled Kandahar. They were flawed human beings. But they knew everyone. The international press corps knew local military commanders, generals and ordinary soldiers. Their local fixers, typically young men, were connected to family and friends and other civilians across the region. They were connected to American and American-allied military spokespeople and officers who used them as propaganda stenographers. The good ones also knew the "bad guys": the Taliban and other militant jihadis fighting to liberate Afghanistan from occupying forces called them from their satellite phones. And because they hung out at hotels like this, they had breakfast next to, and often with, contractors and arms dealers.

Not many people operate at the intersection of so many forces simultaneously interdependent yet in direct conflict as do war reporters. It wouldn't take much for someone who became unmoored from their ethical systems to go rogue. It wouldn't be hard for them to unleash untold mayhem.

"Creative destruction" sounds innocuous. Sort of like letting journalism just wither away. But throwing human beings into the trash of economic history isn't merely cruel, it's unwise, especially when they serve an invaluable role in society. "The Stringer" is both a present and future cautionary tale as well as prediction.

THE CHRISTCHURCH STAR
KENNEDY SHOT DEAD
Gunned Down During Drive Through Dallas
ENLIGHTENED AND FIRM ACTION WAS HIS MARK
The New York Times
MEN WALK ON MOON
ASTRONAUTS LAND ON PLAIN; COLLECT ROCKS, PLANT FLAG
The New York Times
NIXON RESIGNS
HE URGES A TIME OF 'HEALING'; FORD WILL TAKE OFFICE TODAY

I

MY NAME IS
MARK SCRIBNER.
I AM
A JOURNALIST.
JOURNALISM
IS MY LIFE.

JOURNALISM CAN SAVE THE WORLD.

IT'S THE ONLY THING THAT CAN.

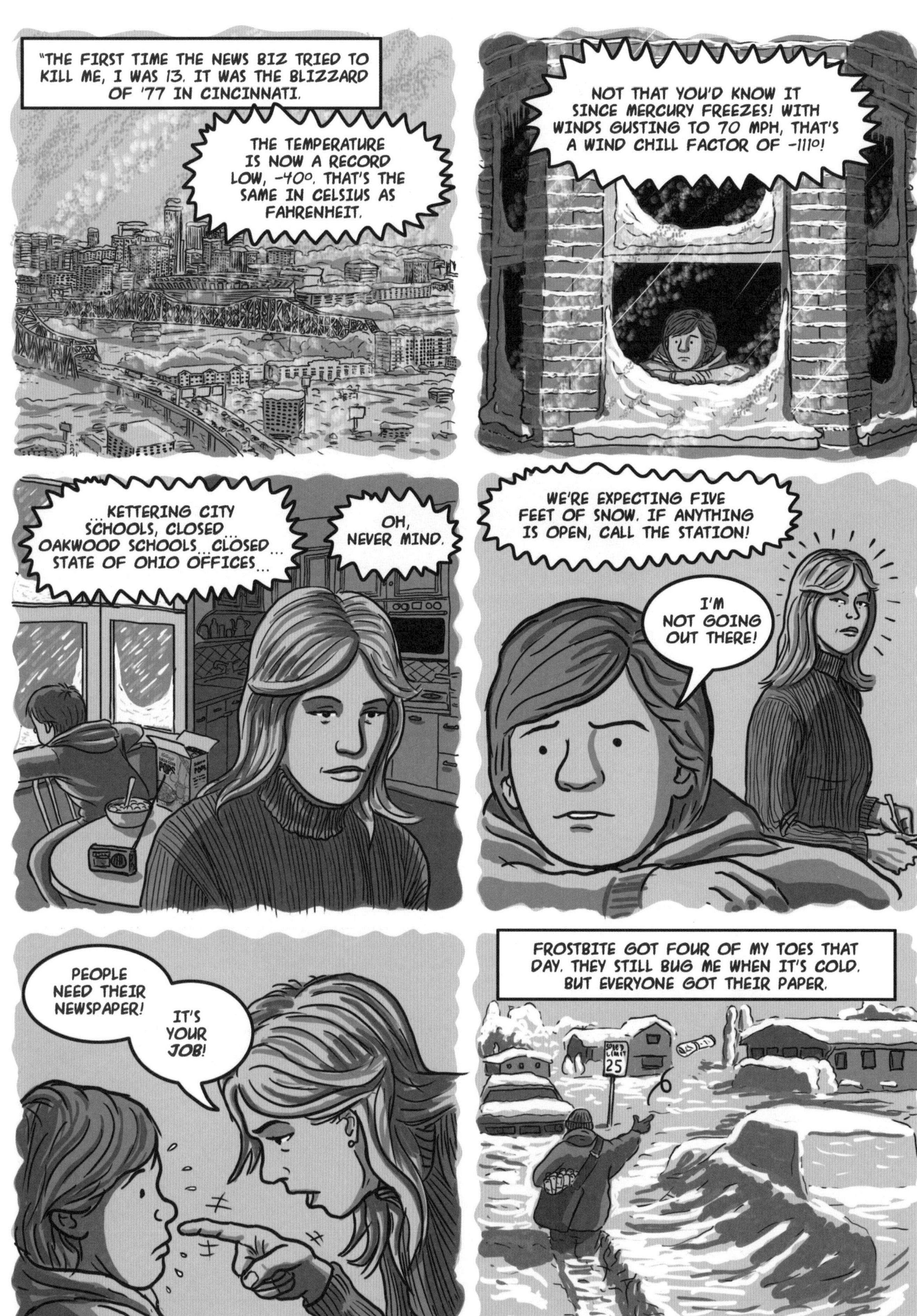
"THE FIRST TIME THE NEWS BIZ TRIED TO KILL ME, I WAS 13. IT WAS THE BLIZZARD OF '77 IN CINCINNATI.
THE TEMPERATURE IS NOW A RECORD LOW, -40°. THAT'S THE SAME IN CELSIUS AS FAHRENHEIT.
NOT THAT YOU'D KNOW IT SINCE MERCURY FREEZES! WITH WINDS GUSTING TO 70 MPH, THAT'S A WIND CHILL FACTOR OF -111°!
...KETTERING CITY SCHOOLS, CLOSED... OAKWOOD SCHOOLS...CLOSED... STATE OF OHIO OFFICES...
OH, NEVER MIND.
WE'RE EXPECTING FIVE FEET OF SNOW. IF ANYTHING IS OPEN, CALL THE STATION!
I'M NOT GOING OUT THERE!
PEOPLE NEED THEIR NEWSPAPER!
IT'S YOUR JOB!
FROSTBITE GOT FOUR OF MY TOES THAT DAY. THEY STILL BUG ME WHEN IT'S COLD. BUT EVERYONE GOT THEIR PAPER.
SPEED LIMIT 25

MY PARENTS WERE DIVORCED IN THAT 1970s TOTAL-WARFARE WAY, UTTER BITTER CONTEMPT FLOWING IN GREAT WAVES OF NASTY LAWYER LETTERS AND "TELL YOUR FATHER/MOTHER" MESSAGES BEFORE AND AFTER COURT-ORDERED VISITATIONS.

THEY DESPISED ONE ANOTHER. BUT THEY BOTH LOVED FILM AND THEY REVERED THE POWER OF THE PRESS.

WHERE'S MY REWRITE ON THE RHINE FIRE?

MARK SCRIBNER, JR.!
GOING TO FOLLOW YOUR FATHER'S FOOTSTEPS?
MAYBE...?

THAT WAS THE LAST THING I WANTED TO DO.

PART OF AN ABANDONED SUBWAY TUNNEL COLLAPSED ON 7th STREET.
I'VE GOT SCHOTTLEKOTE ON IT.
SUBWAYS? IN CINCINNATI?
NEVER COMPLETED. THEY CONVERTED THEM INTO FALLOUT SHELTERS BUT NOW THEY'RE FALLING APART.
IDIOTS. I'LL WRITE AN EDITORIAL CALLING FOR REPAIRS.

THAT WAS MY DAD.

HE CHUCKED ME INTO THE OCEAN.
LIKE A VIKING.
SINK OR SWIM.

ALL THOSE BABIES! DEAD!

POLICE LINE - DO NOT CROSS
CINCINNATI POLICE DEPARTMENT

HELLO, MA'AM. I'M FROM THE POST. WOULD YOU MIND TALKING ABOUT THE FIRE?
REDS

TALK!?!
TIME FOR TALKIN' IS OVER!

3758

SORRY, SIR. I COULDN'T GET THE STORY.
WHY NOT?
NO ONE WOULD TALK TO ME. THEY'RE MAD BECAUSE THE CITY SHUT DOWN THE ONE FIRE STATION IN THE GHETTO.
THEN THAT'S THE STORY.
BLACKS ARE SO PISSED OFF THEY WON'T EVEN TALK TO A WHITE REPORTER.
WRITE IT UP.
DEADLINE! WHERE THE FUCK IS YOUR STORY?
I'M ON MY SECOND DRAFT.
FUCK SECOND DRAFTS!
WHAT YOU WRITE FIRST IS ALWAYS BEST, MOST DRAMATIC.
NEVER SELF-CENSOR.
CENSORSHIP IS MY JOB!

YOUR FATHER HAD TO...
COME ON, KID. I'LL GIVE YOU A RIDE HOME.

SINK OR SWIM.

IF YOU WALK INTO A NEWSROOM TODAY, IT'S STERILE AND QUIET, A TOMB.
INDISTINGUISHABLE FROM AN INSURANCE COMPANY OFFICE OR A BANK.

NEWSROOMS HAD A RHYTHM BACK THEN: THE CLICK-CLACK OF THE WIRE-SERVICE TELETYPE MACHINE, OCCASIONALLY PUNCTUATED BY BELLS THAT SIGNALED IMPORTANT BREAKING NEWS. HUNGOVER GUYS BANGED AWAY ON ANCIENT TYPEWRITERS. NOT LIKE NOW WITH QUIET LITTLE KEYBOARDS.

HOLD PAGE ONE—THE U.S. EMBASSY IN TEHRAN HAS BEEN TAKEN OVER!

10

LISTEN TO THIS D-DAY REPORT:
"THE EYES OF THE WORLD REMAIN RIVETED ON THE BEACHES OF NORMANDY, WHERE ONE OF THE DECISIVE BATTLES OF HISTORY IS NOW GETTING UNDER WAY. BOTH SIDES AGREE THAT GRIM AND BITTER FIGHTING IS RAGING ALONG A STILL INTERMITTENT AND CONFUSED, BUT STEADILY EXPANDING, FRONT..."
THERE'S EVERYTHING YOU NEED TO KNOW.
THE "LEDE": WHAT'S HAPPENING.
WHY THE STORY MATTERS: "THE NUT GRAF."
DESCRIBED IN SIMPLE TERMS THAT DESCRIBE NOT JUST WHAT'S GOING ON, BUT WHAT IT FEELS LIKE!

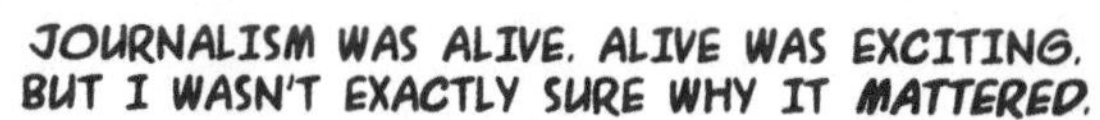
JOURNALISM WAS ALIVE. ALIVE WAS EXCITING. BUT I WASN'T EXACTLY SURE WHY IT MATTERED.

I FOUND THAT OUT AT MY LITTLE HIGH SCHOOL NEWSPAPER.
SPORTS IS DONE.
I WISH WE DIDN'T HAVE TO HAVE STUPID SPORTS.
DRAGON TALES

IT BEGAN WITH AN ANNOUNCEMENT.
IN ORDER TO ADDRESS THE PROBLEM OF DRUGS AND OTHER CONTRABAND BEING BROUGHT TO SCHOOL, WE ARE HOLDING HOMEROOM OVER 20 EXTRA MINUTES TO ALLOW FOR RANDOM SEARCHES OF STUDENT LOCKERS.

I WAS APPALLED BY THIS LATEST CRACKDOWN IN THE SCHOOL ADMINISTRATION'S ONGOING "ASSERTIVE DISCIPLINE" CAMPAIGN — PART OF THE "TOUGH LOVE" ANTI-KID ASSHOLERY OF THE 1970s AND 1980s. BUT I WASN'T PERSONALLY WORRIED. UNLIKE MOST OF MY FRIENDS, I DIDN'T DO POT OR LUDES.

THE POLICE CAME! THEY ARRESTED JIM PATTERSON!
FOR WHAT?
THEY FOUND LIKE A TON OF WEED IN HIS LOCKER.
I DON'T KNOW HIM. BUT... ARRESTED?!

THE KIDS CAUGHT UP IN WAR ON DRUGS/EVIL TEENS HYSTERIA DISAPPEARED INTO THE SYSTEM, GROUND UP BY SHOWBOATING "TOUGH ON CRIME" JUDGES.
YOU ARE HEREBY REMANDED TO THE OHIO STATE PENITENTIARY AT COLUMBUS FOR NOT LESS THAN 30 DAYS. SPEND THAT TIME THINKING ABOUT HOW YOU SPREAD DEATH TO YOUR FELLOW STUDENTS.
BUT YOUR HONOR, HE'S A CHILD—
ADULT CRIME, ADULT TIME!

ONE WEEK LATER:

DAYTON MALL

SOME PRISONER DEFINITELY KNOWS SOMETHING.
BRING CIGARETTES.

I WAS SCARED.
OF COURSE I WAS SCARED.
12

BUT I WAS EVEN ANGRIER ABOUT WHAT HAD HAPPENED TO JAMES THAN I WAS SCARED.
IF THERE'S A HOSTAGE SITUATION, WE WILL NOT RESPOND.
WE WILL NOT NEGOTIATE FOR YOUR RELEASE.
DO YOU UNDERSTAND?
YO.
YO.
I'VE GOT SOMETHING FOR YOU.
YOU HAVE A CAMERA?
WHATCHA GOT FOR ME?
13

Fairmont West
High School
Home of the Dragons

YO.
YO.

$20 FOR A VELOX SEEMS CRAZY.
IT'S WORTH IT.
THE CLASH
DRAGON TALES
EXCLUSIVE:

?

"MURDERED"?
THE DRAGON TALES
EXCLUSIVE:
MURDERED BY THE SCHOOL ADMINISTRATION
FRANK MAN
PRINCIP

YOU SEARCHED HIS LOCKER. YOU TURNED HIM OVER TO THE COPS. THEY SENT HIM TO DIE.
YEAH. YOU KILLED HIM. YOU'RE A FUCKING MURDERER.
14

NEEDLESS TO SAY, I PAID A PRICE.

THE BOARD AFFIRMS THAT 10 DAYS SUSPENSION IS APPROPRIATE. YOU WILL NOT MARCH AT GRADUATION. FURTHER, YOU ARE HEREBY REMOVED FROM THE STAFF OF DRAGON TALES FOR THE DURATION OF YOUR TIME AT FAIRMONT.

SCHOOL COUNSELOR

THEY ORDERED ME TO SEND YOUR DISCIPLINARY RECORD TO THE COLLEGES THAT ACCEPTED YOU.
BUT I "FORGOT" THE IVIES.

BUT IT WASN'T ALL BAD.
Dayton Daily News

Dayton Daily News
DA Investigating State Pen Teen Death.
Attorney general to provide new evidences
Dayton Daily

THANK YOU, MARK. BECAUSE OF YOU, THEY COULDN'T BURY THIS.
WE'RE SUING SO THEY CAN'T DO THIS TO ANY MORE KIDS.
15

HELP
SCHOOL COUNSELOR
THE COLUMBIA SCHOLASTIC PRESS ASSOCIATION IN THE CITY OF NEW YORK IS PROUD TO AWARD ITS CROWN AWARD FOR OVERALL EXCELLENCE TO...
YOU, MARK.
WELCOME ABOARD, STAFF REPORTER SCRIBNER!
YOUR DESK WILL BE WAITING FOR YOU WHEN YOU COME BACK FROM NEW YORK.
IT'S A MIRACLE! WE'RE BOTH GOING TO THE SAME COLLEGE!
THEY HAVE A DORM FOR MARRIED COUPLES...
WOULD ENGAGED COUNT?
COLUMBIA UNIVERSITY IN THE CITY OF NEW YORK
16

AMSTERDAM AV

THE LIBRARY OF COLUMBIA UNIVERSITY

COLUMBIA SPECTATOR

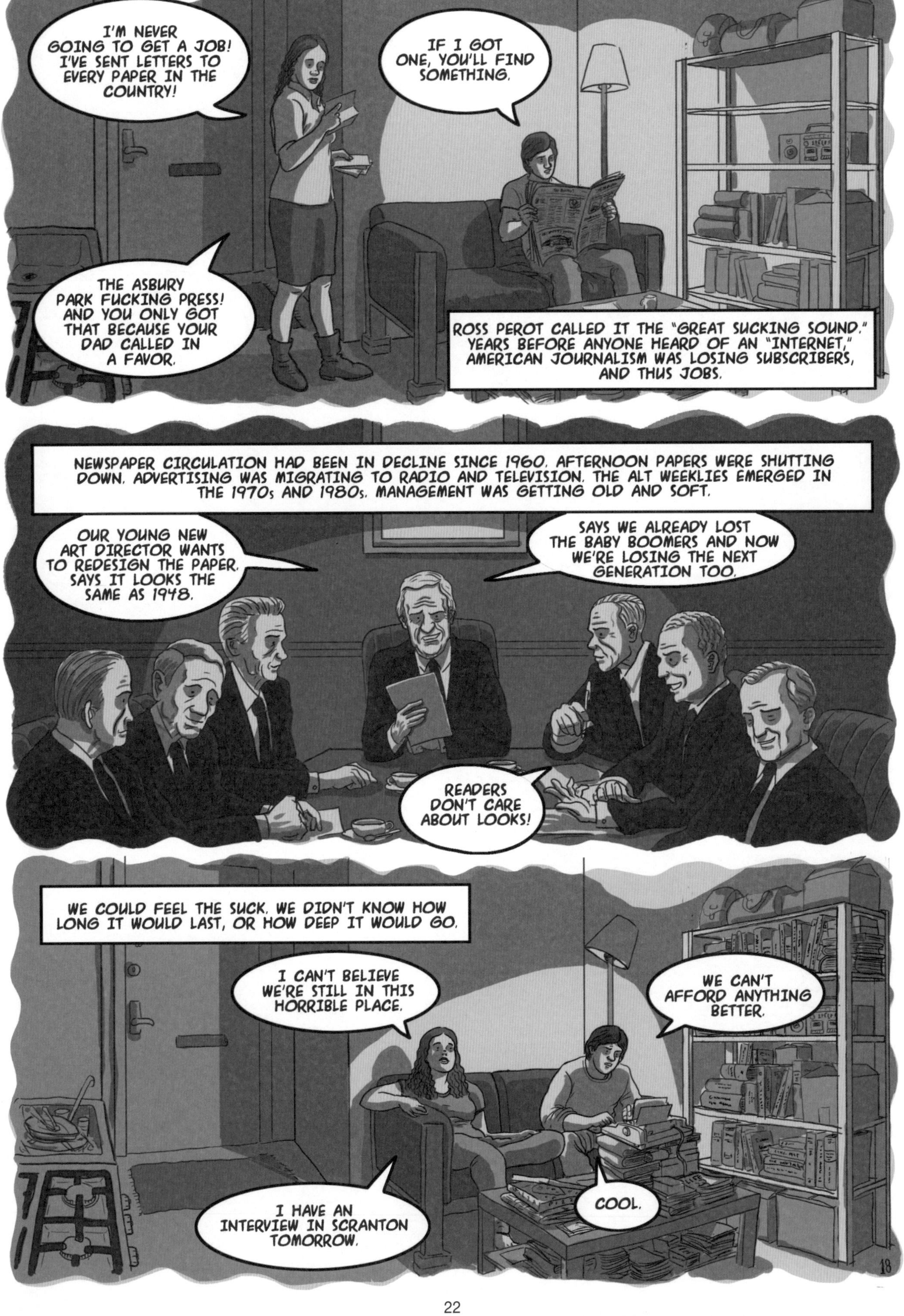

NEWSPAPER CIRCULATION HAD BEEN IN DECLINE SINCE 1960. AFTERNOON PAPERS WERE SHUTTING DOWN. ADVERTISING WAS MIGRATING TO RADIO AND TELEVISION. THE ALT WEEKLIES EMERGED IN THE 1970s AND 1980s. MANAGEMENT WAS GETTING OLD AND SOFT.

OUR YOUNG NEW ART DIRECTOR WANTS TO REDESIGN THE PAPER. SAYS IT LOOKS THE SAME AS 1948.

SAYS WE ALREADY LOST THE BABY BOOMERS AND NOW WE'RE LOSING THE NEXT GENERATION TOO.

READERS DON'T CARE ABOUT LOOKS!

WE COULD FEEL THE SUCK. WE DIDN'T KNOW HOW LONG IT WOULD LAST, OR HOW DEEP IT WOULD GO.

I CAN'T BELIEVE WE'RE STILL IN THIS HORRIBLE PLACE.

WE CAN'T AFFORD ANYTHING BETTER.

I HAVE AN INTERVIEW IN SCRANTON TOMORROW.

COOL.

AND NOW THERE'S HAIL... I CAN'T HARDLY SEE ANYTHING.

WALL ST. PANIC
by Mark Scribner
What happened yesterday in the

MARK, I'M SORRY.
THERE'S BEEN AN ACCIDENT.

YOU CAN TAKE THE CALL IN MY OFFICE.

THE COLUMBIA SCHOLAST
PRESS ASSOCIATION IN THE
OF NEW YORK
is proud to award its
CROWN AWARD FOR OVERALL EXC
to
Mark Scribner
Given at Columbia University in the City of New

SUMMA CUM LAUDE. COULDN'T FIND A JOB.
THAT'S WHY SHE WAS SCHLEPPING OUT TO PENNSYLVANIA FOR SOME SHIT LITTLE JOB AT SOME SHIT LITTLE PAPER.
MEANWHILE THESE CORPORATE RAIDERS ARE SCOOPING UP PAPERS AND CONSOLIDATING THEM AND PAYING THEMSELVES TENS OF MILLIONS OF DOLLARS FOR DOING NOTHING.
HEY, MAN, HELP ME OUT?
HOMELESS NEED YOUR HELP $ $$
OPEN
FUCK YOU!
OPEN
ONE WAY

NEXT CAME THE INTERNET.
YOU'RE TELLING US THAT WE SHOULD JUST SPOONFEED READERS WITH WHAT THEY WANT. TO GET CLICKS. BUT READERS WANT KITTENS AND PUPPIES.
FUCK YOU AND YOUR JOURNALISTIC ARROGANCE OF DECIDING THAT KITTENS AND PUPPIES AREN'T IMPORTANT.
HOPEFULLY WE GET TO THE POINT WHERE OUR REVENUE IS SO SIGNIFICANT THAT WE CAN DO PUPPIES **AND** AFGHANISTAN, OKAY?
OH, AND: FUCK YOU!
IT WAS HARD TO DECIDE WHICH WAS WORSE. GETTING LAID OFF?
The Orlando Sentinel
OR **NOT** GETTING LAID OFF?
Los Angeles Times
INVESTIGATIVE JOURNALISM?
THAT TAKES MONTHS AND TENS OF THOUSANDS OF DOLLARS.
FOR 5000 WORDS AND MAYBE A PULITZER NO ONE GIVES A SHIT ABOUT. WE CAN'T AFFORD THAT ANYMORE.
CORRUPT POLITICIANS HAVE WON, MARK. IF YOU WANT TO KEEP WORKING HERE, YOU'RE GOING TO HAVE TO GET STUFF NO ONE ELSE CAN GET.
IN THE FIELD.
GUSHY STUFF.

GUSHY STUFF.
BRRAM

BRAMM
PRESS
PRESS

BRAAM
BRRAAM
THIS WAY!
PRESS

SAY THIS FOR THE GUSHY STUFF:
PRESS

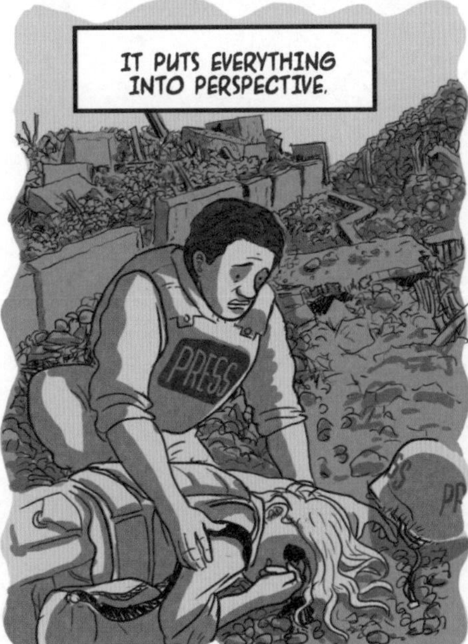
IT PUTS EVERYTHING INTO PERSPECTIVE.
PRESS

KILL OR BE KILLED. SINK OR SWIM.

NOTHING CAN SAVE THE WORLD.

ESPECIALLY NOT JOURNALISM.

THINGS WERE CHANGING FAST. MILLENNIALS SEEMED TO GET IT.

SO I MADE FRIENDS WITH MILLENNIALS.

I'M SORRY, MARK. THE WORLD IS COMING TO AN END.
DON'T BE SORRY. IT'S NOT YOUR FAULT.

EDITORS HAVE ALWAYS BEEN CHEAP. PUBLISHERS HAVE ALWAYS BEEN STUPID. GETTING FIRED COMES WITH THE TERRITORY WHEN YOU'RE FREELANCE.
BUT WHAT WE DO IS IMPORTANT.

NOW THEY'RE GIVING NEWS AWAY ONLINE AND THEY'RE SURPRISED THEY'RE NOT MAKING ANY MONEY. ANY HOOKER KNOWS BETTER THAN TO GIVE AWAY THEIR PRODUCT FOR FREE.
WHAT YOU DO IS IMPORTANT.

IT USED TO BE. BUT DON'T THINK I DON'T APPRECIATE YOUR VALUE SYSTEM, MARGREET. I REALLY DO.
26

POOR GIRL... STILL THINKS IT'S POSSIBLE TO MAKE THE WORLD A BETTER PLACE.

THE NEW CHINESE KNOCKOFFS ARE GETTING BETTER.

MOM ALWAYS SAID I SHOULD'VE GONE INTO ARMS SALES.

PRESS

IS THAT IT? ARE YOU GOING TO GO HOME?
Dushanbe, Tajikstan
210 kilometers north of Afghanistan

YEAH, CAN'T WAIT. IT'S SO FUN AND AWESOME BACK THERE.
Ding!

OF COURSE I DIDN'T SEND THE RENT CHECK. THERE'S NO MONEY IN OUR ACCOUNT. DO YOU UNDERSTAND THAT?
YOU'RE A FAILURE! USELESS! NO ONE WANTS YOU! I DON'T WANT YOU!

FUCK YOU! THEY READ ME AT THE WHITE HOUSE. I'VE WRITTEN BOOKS. MY "FAILURES" ARE BIGGER THAN THE BIGGEST SUCCESSES YOU COULD EVER DREAM OF!

SO THEN, WHAT NEXT?
"AT A PRESS CONFERENCE IN BANGUI, CENTRAL AFRICAN REPUBLIC PRIME MINISTER MARTIN ZIGUELE SAID THAT CHADIAN SOLDIERS PENETRATED 7 KILOMETERS INTO HIS COUNTRY ON AUGUST 6...
28

... AND ATTACKED GOVERNMENT TROOPS WITH GROUND-TO-GROUND MISSILES, TANKS AND HEAVY ARTILLERY, STATE-OWNED RADIO CENTRAFRIQUE REPORTED."
GOOD FUN.

NO ONE CARES. NO ONE IS GOING TO THE FUCKING C.A.R.
IF A PLATOON FALLS IN THE WOODS —OR DOWN THE STREET— DOES IT MAKE A SOUND?
NOT IF THERE ISN'T A REPORTER THERE.

THAT'S THE OLD WORLD. NOW EVERYTHING IS VIRTUAL. EVEN WAR.
CYBERWARRIORS HACK INTO IRAN'S NUKES TO FUCK WITH THEM.

IMAGES FLASHED AROUND THE WORLD ON FACEBOOK.
MORE PEOPLE FOLLOW TWITTER THAN READ THE NEW YORK TIMES AND EVERY OTHER NEWSPAPER COMBINED.

BY THE TIME WE PARACHUTE INTO A WAR ZONE, CITIZEN JOUNALISTS HAVE ALREADY BLOGGED ALL THE BEST PHOTOS AND POSTED VIDEOS AND TOLD THE WORLD WHAT'S GOING ON.
ALL FOR FREE.

JOURNALISM IS OBSOLETE.
WAIT—LET ME RESTATE THAT. JOURNALISTS ARE OBSOLETE.
STILL GOING TO AFGHANISTAN?

STILL WORKING ON FINDING A NEW FIXER.

TOO BAD ABOUT JOVID. HE WAS A GOOD KID.

MQ-9 Reaper control room, 432nd Air Expeditionary Wing, Creech Air Force Base, Indian Springs, Nevada

WELL, GOOD NIGHT.
Ding!

SURPRISE, SURPRISE. THEY'RE OFFERING ME MY OLD JOB BACK.
LET ME GUESS: FREELANCE, PAY CUT, NO BENEFITS, THEY'VE ALREADY RESERVED YOU A ONE-WAY TO BANGUI.

YOU'RE PSYCHIC!
PSYCHO IS MORE LIKE IT. HAVE FUN IN LA BELLE AFRIQUE.

31

WHAT'S CHANGED IS THE BUSINESS OF WAR: HOW IT STARTS (THE PROVOCATION), HOW IT'S MARKETED (THE PROPAGANDA), WHO PROFITS AND BENEFITS (WHICH CORPORATIONS, WHICH POLITICIANS). THE VIRTUAL SPACE—THE INTERNET—IS THE FOURTH DIMENSION OF THE POSTMODERN BATTLEFIELD.

AN ANONYMOUS REMAILING PROGRAM ALLOWS A USER TO SEND AN EMAIL THAT LOOKS LIKE IT CAME FROM YOUR EMAIL ADDRESS.

THERE'S NO WAY TO TELL WHO REALLY WROTE IT.
larry70@vptn.com
To: clairearhome@vptn.com
Miss U :)

AMAZING HOW MANY BADASS WARLORDS USE EMAIL.
AMAZING HOW FEW KNOW ABOUT BASIC HACKING TOOLS.

YOU CAN DO THE SAME THING WITH PHONE TEXTING.
THIRD-PARTY SERVICES LIKE SPOOFCARD LET YOU DO "CALLER ID SPOOFING"—USE YOUR PHONE TO SEND A TEXT MESSAGE THAT LOOKS EXACTLY LIKE IT CAME FROM ANY PHONE NUMBER OF YOUR CHOOSING.

SOCIAL MEDIA IS EVEN EASIER.
CREATE USERNAME
Add a username or use our suggestion. You can change this at any time.
presidentmacron-france
MANY PUBLIC FIGURES DON'T HAVE TWITTER OR FACEBOOK ACCOUNTS.
ANYONE CAN REGISTER THEIR NAME AND START POSTING INFLAMMATORY STATEMENTS.

IT DOESN'T OCCUR TO ANYONE THAT THE ACCOUNT MIGHT NOT BE AUTHENTIC.

OF COURSE, MANY OTHER FIGURES DO HAVE WELL-ESTABLISHED SOCIAL MEDIA PRESENCES.
BUT SO WHAT?
Donald Trump @realmrdonaldjtrump - 38m
So much sex with Melania, so great!
6.4K 3.5K 18K
Donald Trump @realmrdonaldjtrump
FAKE NEWS MEDIA.
ALL YOU HAVE TO DO IS CREATE AN IDENTITY CLOSE ENOUGH TO THE GENUINE ARTICLE TO SEEM PLAUSIBLE.

KIDS HACKED EACH OTHER'S IDENTITIES FOR FUN, AS PRANKS. WHEN ADULTS DID IT, IT WAS USUALLY FOR REVENGE.
GO SLEEP WITH YOUR SLUT!

NOT ME. I WAS OUT TO CHANGE THE WORLD.
BUT HOW?

SOMETIMES—YOU KNOW THE FEELING—SOMETHING JUST COMES OVER YOU.
Join Twitter today.
Full name
Email address
Create a password
Choose your username

INSPIRATION? WHO KNOWS?
Choose your username
@IshmaelKhan
TAP TAP TAP TAP TAP

Cancel
New Tweet
@IshmaelKhan: To hell with apostate dog @RashidDostum, scum of Mazar
TAP TAP TAP TAP TAP TAP TAP TAP

IN THE 21ST CENTURY, EVERYONE IS ONLINE—EVEN WARLORDS.
Abdul Rashid Dostum, ethnic Uzbek, leader of Junbish-e Milli-yi Islam-yi Afghanistan, Chairman of Joint Chiefs of the Afghan National Army, Warlord of Mazar-i-Sharif, NE Afghanistan

IT TURNS OUT THAT A SOCIETY BUILT ON TRIBALISM AND ANCIENT RITUALS OF HONOR IS EASILY PUNK'D.
Mohammed Ishmael Khan, ethnic Tajik, leader of Jamiat-e Islami, Minister of Water and Energy, Warlord of Herat, NW Afghanistan

BRING-BRING
BRING-BRING
BRING-BRING

WHAT?
YEAH, I CAN BE THERE THIS AFTERNOON. I'M RIGHT ACROSS THE BORDER.

NEWS
AFGHANISTAN: ANOTHER CIVIL WAR?
WE ARE GETTING SKETCHY REPORTS OF ROCKET FIRE EXCHANGED BETWEEN FORCES LOYAL TO GENERALS KHAN AND DOSTUM NEAR THE PROVINCIAL BORDER TOWN OF MAIMANA.
JESUS.

MY FIRST BONAFIDE SCOOP. WHICH I MADE HAPPEN.
LIVE
MAIMANA, AFGHANISTAN
HE SAYS WE CAN HAVE IT FOR $100,000, TAKE IT OR LEAVE IT.
TAKE IT. HE'S THE ONLY ONE THERE. IF WE PASS, HE SELLS IT TO MSNBC OR FOX.
THE BATTLE OF MAIMANA WAS DRAMATIC, VISUALLY ARRESTING, AND—MOST IMPORTANTLY—FUNDED MY DIVORCE.
36

AFTER WHAT I'D BEEN THROUGH, WHY SUCCUMB TO SCRUPLES?
TWICE THE WINNER OF THE OVERSEAS PRESS CLUB AWARD, IN 1991 AND 1993, MARK SCRIBNER'S INTIMATE AND HUMANE COVERAGE OF THE MAY...
Columbia Journalism School
MAY?
MAINAMA CONFLICT —DID I PRONOUNCE THAT CORRECTLY?— WON THIS YEAR'S PULITZER PRIZE.

I HADN'T MERELY BREACHED JOURNALISM'S MOST SACRED TENETS. I'D RAPED THE SHIT OUT OF THEM.
A GOOD WAR REPORTER NEEDS TWO THINGS: GUTS AND LUCK.
MARK SCRIBNER HAS ENOUGH OF THE FORMER, AND TONS OF THE LATTER.
WHEN WAR BREAKS OUT, MARK IS USUALLY THERE —OFTENTIMES BEFORE IT STARTS.
60 MINUTES

THANKS FOR COMING, MARK.
THANKS, CHRISTIANE. BIG FAN.
37

I USED TO HATE PLAGIARISTS.
BUT WHO WAS I TO JUDGE THEM?
COPYING SOMEONE ELSE'S CRAP WAS PUSSY SHIT NEXT TO STARTING A WAR.
SOLDIERS LOYAL TO DEPOSED FORMER PRESIDENT MARC RAVALOMANANA, WHO HAD FORESWORN POLITICS...
... BUT ARE SAID TO HAVE BEEN PROVOKED BY UNSOURCED LIBELOUS STATEMENTS ATTRIBUTED TO HERY RAJAONARIMAMPIANINA...
... HAVE SEIZED GOVERNMENT BUILDINGS IN THE CAPITAL.
NOT A BIG WAR, MIND YOU. BUT STILL.

STEPHEN GLASS AND JASON BLAIR WERE THE WORST JOURNO-CRIMINALS EVER. BUT EVEN THEY WERE JUST FABULISTS. THEY MADE UP STORIES FROM WHOLE CLOTH. BETTER THAN THAN UNLEASHING THE HORRORS OF WAR —HORRORS WHICH I KNEW BETTER THAN ALMOST ANYONE.
TWICE THE WINNER OF THE PULITZER PRIZE...
NATIONAL PRESS CLUB

... MARK SCRIBNER—

PLAGIARISTS HAD NOTHING ON ME.

BECAUSE OF ME, HUNDREDS —POSSIBLY THOUSANDS— OF PEOPLE WERE DEAD.

I MIGHT AS WELL HAVE SHOT THEM MYSELF.
MEDIUM SCRAMBLED, SLIGHTLY CRISPY ON THE EDGES.
39

I FELT GUILTY—FOR NOT FEELING GUILTY.

MY DAD WOULDN'T HAVE APPROVED.
THERE IS NO TRUTH.
THE CLOSEST YOU CAN GET TO TRUTH IS ROUGH APPROXIMATION.
BUT THERE IS HONESTY. WE OWE THE READERS THAT.
LET THEM KNOW HOW THE SAUSAGE IS MADE SO THEY CAN EAT IT WITH EYES OPEN, OR THROW THE ROTTEN MEAT AWAY.
A DISHONEST REPORTER —WHETHER HE LIES OUTRIGHT OR VIA OMISSION— IS SCUM.
THAT'S FOR DAMN SURE.

Autonomous vehicle command center, Doshan Tapeh Air Base, outside Tehran
ARE YOU SURE ABOUT THIS TARGET?
ENCRYPTED, BUT MISIRI SAYS IT'S ALWAYS BEEN RELIABLE.

FUCK GUILT.
40

INTELLECTUALLY, OF COURSE, I KNEW THAT WHAT I WAS DOING WAS "WRONG."
WE'LL UPLOAD THE B-ROLL AS SOON AS I ARRIVE AT THE NAMIBIAN—ANGOLAN BORDER.
CNN
LOOK FOR SOME ETHNIC CLEANSING-Y STUFF FROM ME BY FRIDAY, MONDAY AT THE LATEST.
HOW DO YOU KNOW?
HAVE I EVER LET YOU DOWN?

THIS IS WNYC FM, LIVE FROM NEW YORK CITY. SIMULTANEOUS SUICIDE BOMBS STRUCK THREE OPEN-AIR MARKETS IN KARACHI.

AUTHORITIES BLAME ISLAMIC MILITANTS, BUT NO GROUP HAS CLAIMED RESPONSIBILITY.

AT&T
11:23
84%
Message
Encrypted
Cancel
Send
To: pm-netanyahu@gov.is
Cc:
Bcc:
Subject:
72 hours to release our prisoners or we will execute Israeli POWs on Gaza TV
TAP TAP
TAP
TAP
TAP TAP
space
.123

WHAT A WORLD! DO YOU THINK THERE WILL EVER BE PEACE?
NOT AS LONG AS THERE'S MONEY TO BE MADE.
EVERY NOW AND THEN—JUST WHEN I WAS STARTING TO QUESTION MYSELF—SOMETHING WOULD HAPPEN TO RESTORE MY SENSE OF ENTITLEMENT.

Belt Pkwy WEST
Kennedy Airport
WEST 27 No Conduit Ave
NORTH
Van Wyck Expwy
Whitestone Bridge
BEEP
BEEP
BEEP
BEEP

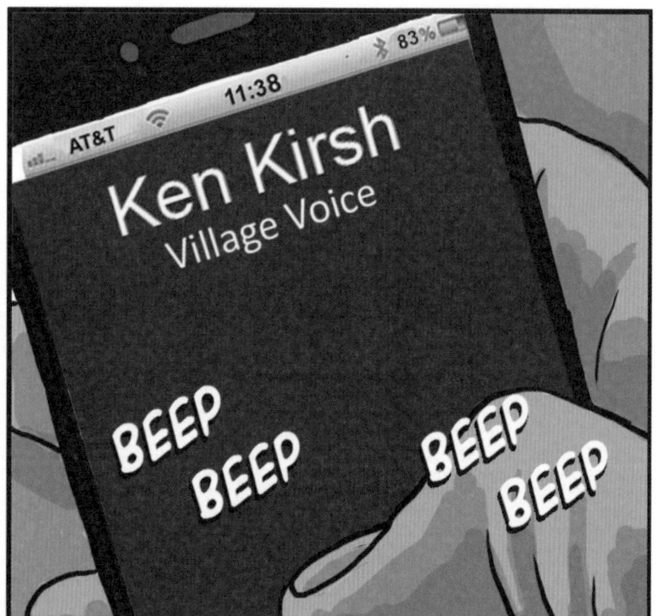
AT&T
11:38
83%
Ken Kirsh
Village Voice
BEEP
BEEP
BEEP
BEEP

KEN.

VOICE
VOICE
Make Love, Not War
MARK SCRIBNER! LONG TIME!
HOW ARE YOU? HOW'S THAT WIFE OF YOURS?

WHAT CAN I DO FOR YOU, KEN?

VOICE
BOTH THE WRITERS I ASSIGNED TO GET INTO MOLDOVA FLAKED OUT. WANNA GO?

ON MY WAY TO AFRICA, BUT I COULD STOP ON THE WAY OVER OR BACK.
HOW MANY WORDS?
HOW MUCH YOU PAYING?

I COULD USE 1,500 WORDS. 2,000 IF YOU CAN FIND SOME INSIDE DISH FROM THE FSB.
FILE ON SPEC. IF I USE IT, I PAY 10 CENTS A WORD.

...
YOU THERE?

MARK?
ARE YOU SERIOUS?
YOU WANT TO PAY ME —ANYONE— $150?
ON SPEC?
CHECK YOUR BAGGAGE HERE

I COULD GET FUCKING KILLED OVER THERE, YOU ASSHOLE!

PRESS
TV

MAGAZINES
BOOKS
BOOKS
OBVIOUSLY YOU HAVEN'T BEEN KEEPING UP WITH CURRENT EVENTS.

COLUMBIA JOURNALISM REVIEW
The Second Coming of War Correspondency
Mark Scribner talks about the new journalism
MY FEE FOR SOMETHING LIKE THIS STARTS AT $50,000.

I DON'T HAVE THE BUDGET—
THEN YOU'RE GOING TO GO OUT OF BUSINESS.

THAT FUCKING HAG ARIANNA HUFFINGTON DOESN'T KNOW IT YET, BUT HER SCREW-THE-WRITERS MODEL IS DEAD.
CONTENT IS KING AGAIN!

TOO MANY ONLINE DOLLARS CHASING TOO MANY READERS, BUT THERE ARE MORE OUTLETS THAN TALENTED JOURNALISTS TO PROVIDE THEM WITH CONTENT.
YOU WANT REAL REPORTING BY REAL WRITERS, YOU'RE GOING TO HAVE TO PAY REAL MONEY.
45

F 28
AF8985
15:35
DAKAR
ON TIME
NOT OLD REAL MONEY.
NEW REAL MONEY!

SENEGAL
6V-AII

FOR 15 LONG YEARS, REPORTERS HAD WORKED LIKE DOGS FOR EDITORS WHO TREATED THEM LIKE SHIT.

LOW PAY, DISRESPECT, AND REPEATEDLY GETTING LAID OFF SO SOME SENIOR VICE PRESIDENT IN AN AIR-CONDITIONED OFFICE COULD GET A SEVEN-FIGURE RAISE.

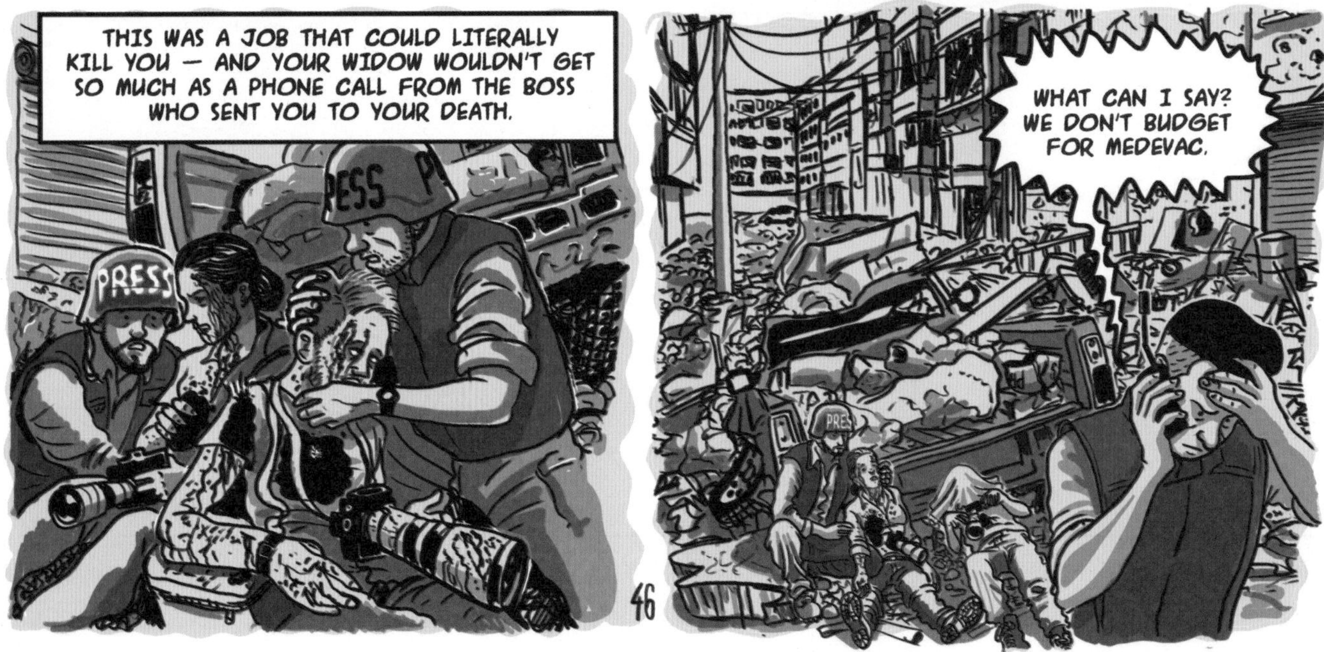
THIS WAS A JOB THAT COULD LITERALLY KILL YOU — AND YOUR WIDOW WOULDN'T GET SO MUCH AS A PHONE CALL FROM THE BOSS WHO SENT YOU TO YOUR DEATH.
PRESS
PRESS
WHAT CAN I SAY? WE DON'T BUDGET FOR MEDEVAC.
46

SHE DIED GETTING THAT STORY.
NOW YOU'RE GIVING IT AWAY ONLINE.
FOR FREE.
I HEAR WHAT YOU'RE SAYING. WE'RE TESTING A PAYWALL MODEL... MAYBE $30 A MONTH.
2015
PRINT DOLLARS HAVE BEEN REPLACED BY DIGITAL PENNIES. AD RATES HAVE HIT ROCK BOTTOM.
WE HAVE 13 MILLION READERS ONLINE AND 1 MILLION IN PRINT, AND WE EARN 13 TIMES MORE FROM PRINT THAN THE WEB EDITION.
FOR THE TIMES, AN ONLINE READER IS WORTH 1/169TH AS MUCH AS A PRINT ONE — AND THAT'S THE FUTURE.
YOU CAN'T REPLACE 1 MILLION PRINT READERS WITH 169 MILLION ONLINE ONES.
NEVER HAPPEN.
47

NOBODY KNOWS HOW TO MONETIZE THE INTERNET.
WE ASSUME THERE'S A FUTURE — BUT WE DON'T KNOW.
IN THE MEANTIME, WE CLOSE FOREIGN BUREAUS.
WE LAY OFF REPORTERS. WE RELY ON WIRE SERVICE STUFF AND LOCAL STRINGERS.
WE REPLACE EXPERIENCED JOURNALISTS WITH WET-BEHIND-THE-EARS MILLENNIALS WILLING TO WORK FOR "EXPOSURE."
AND NO MEDEVAC.
NO MEDEVACS.
CINDERELLA
TONY AWARDS
EST MUSICAL
Kodak
WICKED
Merrill Lync
Wealth Managem
48

POOR SUITS! IT TOOK THEM AGES TO FIGURE OUT THE INTERNET.
AEROPORT INTERNATIONAL LEOPOLD SEDAR SENGHOR
6V-AN
SCREE!!
SCREE!!

NOT ME.
Dakar City

SOMEDAY, PERHAPS, PEOPLE WOULD PAY SMART PEOPLE TO DO WORTHWHILE THINGS ONLINE.
SOUVENIRS DAKAR
UNTIL THEN, THERE WERE TWO WAYS TO MAKE MONEY ONLINE.

WHAT STARTED AS AGGREGATION —STEALING OTHER PEOPLE'S CONTENT— MORPHED INTO "SELLING" FABRICATED "FAKE NEWS."
News
Top St
NEWS
THE HUF
THE INTERNET NEW
BUSINESS
MEDIA
Business
Sci/Tech
Sports

THEN THERE WAS TROLLING, AKA FUCKING WITH PEOPLE.
Personal reputation solutio
Learn more
NAKEDCELEBS.C
actors
tv
hottest
REMOVEYOURMUGSHOT
ONLY
$50

49

WELL, THERE'S PORN. BUT I WAS TOO OLD FOR THAT. ANYWAY, EVEN TITS AND ASS WERE GETTING SQUEEZED BY DIGITALIZATION.
$250 IS ALL I CAN DO.
A MILLION AMATEURS WITH IPHONES ARE FLOODING THE MARKET.

ME, I WAS IN THE TROLLING BUSINESS.
JUST A SMALL GIFT. YOUR CAMERA?

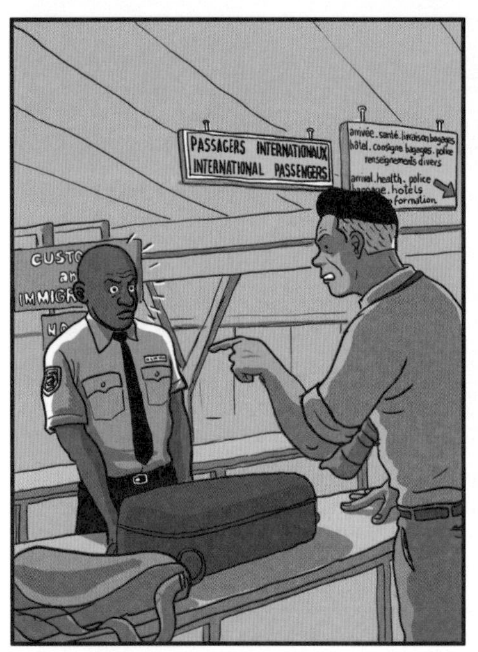
PASSAGERS INTERNATIONAUX
INTERNATIONAL PASSENGERS

PASSAGERS INTERNATIONAUX
INTERNATIONAL PASSENGERS

PASSAGERS INTERNATIONAUX
INTERNATIONAL PASSENGERS

PASSAGERS INTERNATIONAUX
INTERNATIONAL PASSENGERS
50

ISLAMIST TERRORISM TURNS UP IN THE MOST SURPRISING PLACES.
AS DO "TIPS" TO THE AUTHORITIES.

I RATIONALIZED.

THE BIG ACTORS WILL ALWAYS PLAY TO THE MEDIA, MARK. BUT WE MUST NEVER MAKE THE NEWS.
WE'RE NOT THE STORY. WE *TELL* THE STORY.

I WASN'T *CAUSING* WARS. I WAS SPARKING WARS THAT WOULD HAVE HAPPENED ANYWAY, UNDER SLIGHTLY DIFFERENT CIRCUMSTANCES, AT SLIGHTLY DIFFERENT TIMES.

THERE IS *TOO* A DIFFERENCE.
51

NO QUESTION ABOUT IT, I LIT THE MATCH. BUT THE TINDER WAS DRY. THE SPARKS WERE FLYING AROUND. IF IT WASN'T ME AND MY GIFT FOR ENCRYPTION—THANK YOU, EDWARD SNOWDEN!—SOMEONE ELSE WOULD HAVE CASHED IN.

THESE ASSHOLES WOULD HAVE KILLED EACH OTHER ANYWAY. SINCE THE FIREWORKS WERE INEVITABLE, WHY NOT MAKE SURE THEY WENT OFF AT A TIME CONVENIENT TO ME AND MY BOOMING CAREER?
Lieutenant General
John Mutwa
Namibia Defence Force

THE STRATEGIC BORDER CROSSING AT OSHIKANGO LIES IN RUINS TODAY. JUST ANOTHER BORDER SKIRMISH? OR SOMETHING MORE?
EXCLUSIVE
LIVE: MARK SCRIBNE
Namibian authorities say "sit
13:33 CET
TONIGHT, I'LL HAVE AN EXCLUSIVE INTERVIEW WITH THE LEADER OF THE JONAS SAVIMBI SOCIALIST COMMITTEE OF NATIONAL LIBERATION.

THE IDF REFUSES TO CONFIRM OR DENY RESPONSIBILITY FOR THIS AIRSTRIKE IN THE SHEJAIYA NEIGHBORHOOD OF GAZA CITY, BUT THE APPARENT TARGET—A REPLACEMENT BROADCAST FACILITY FOR HAMAS' AL-AQSA STATE TV—LEAVES LITTLE DOUBT AS TO THE ORIGIN OF THE ATTACK. AND YET, AL-AQSA REMAINS ON THE AIR TONIGHT.
52

THANK YOUR SOURCE IN TEL AVIV FOR THE TIP.
NEXT TIME, EUROS OR DOLLARS.

Assignment NAMIBIA: Going Where Other Reporters Are Afraid to Tread
WELCOME TO POWELL'S CITY OF BOOKS
Assignment NAMIBIA: Going Where Other Reporters Are Afraid to Tread
Mark Scribner
PC
PEARL-CONTINENTAL
Lahore
Gather the blessings of Ramadan with your loved ones at the Pearl-Continental Lahore. Diners will be treated to a sumptupus feast of exquisite favorites with "Live Qawali" during the Holy Month.
Please contact reception for details.
IT WAS, AS THE SONG WENT, A VERY GOOD YEAR.

BACK IN THE 1990s, TWO GUYS WROTE A BOOK CALLED "THE WINNER-TAKE-ALL SOCIETY: WHY THE FEW AT THE TOP GET SO MUCH MORE THAN THE REST OF US."

ITS AUTHORS ARGUED THAT, AS ATTENTION SPANS BECAME SHORTER AND MORE MEDIA COMPETED FOR PEOPLE'S ATTENTION, ONLY THE TOP FEW ACHIEVERS IN A PROFESSION WOULD STICK IN THEIR MEMORIES.

THIS TENDENCY WOULD BE SELF-REINFORCED AS THOSE BIG WINNERS COMMANDED MORE MONEY AND FAME ***BECAUSE*** THEY WERE ALREADY RICH AND FAMOUS. IF YOU WERE #1 OR #2 OR MAYBE #3, YOU'D LIVE LIKE A GOD. IF YOU WERE #4, YOU WOULDN'T GET DICK.

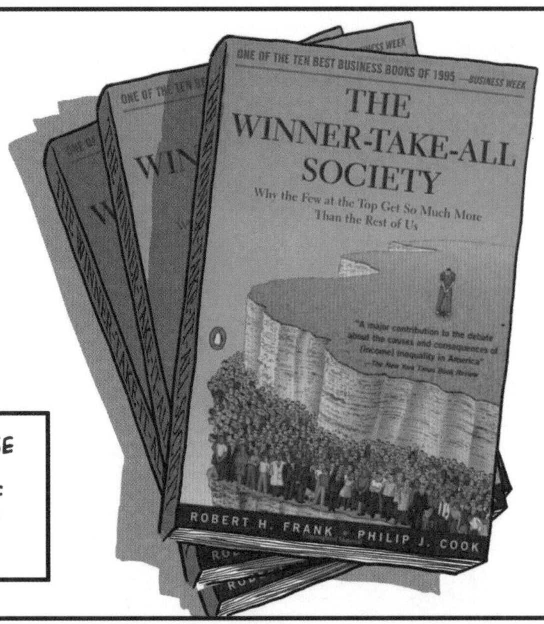

I'D SPENT ALMOST ALL MY LIFE AS NUMBER WHATEVER. IT SUCKED: NEVER ENOUGH MONEY TO MAKE THE BILLS, NEVER ENOUGH STATUS TO COMMAND RESPECT.
Dateline: DAMASCUS
NOW THERE WAS A STRONG CASE FOR ME AS MAYBE THE THIRD MOST SUCCESSFUL CELEBRITY JOURNALIST IN AMERICA—AND I WAS WILLING TO DO JUST ABOUT ANYTHING NOT TO GO BACK TO THE SHITTY OLD DAYS.

BUT THAT WASN'T ENOUGH. LIKE WALTER WHITE IN "BREAKING BAD," I WAS IN THE EMPIRE-BUILDING BUSINESS. I WANTED TO MAKE SO MUCH MONEY, ACCRUE SO MUCH POWER, THAT NO ONE WOULD EVER BE ABLE TO PUT ME BACK IN MY PLACE—AND IF THEY DID (HELLO, DAN RATHER), I'D BE SO FUCKING RICH THAT IT WOULDN'T MATTER.

I HAD THE EXPERIENCE. I HAD THE CONTACTS. I HAD THE KNOWLEDGE. MOST OF ALL, I HAD THE FEAR OF GOING BACK. I HAD EVERYTHING I NEEDED IN ORDER TO BECOME MUCH, MUCH MORE THAN JUST ANOTHER SCHLUB WHO READS THE NEWS INTO A TELEPROMPTER.
I TOOK THE BUYOUT.

2018 PULITZER PRIZE
International Reporting
MARK SCRIBNER
COLUMBIA
JOURNALISM
REVIEW
The Second Coming
of War Correspondency
Mark Scribner talks about the new

III

Pul-e-Charkhi prison, outside Kabul
"JACK" IDEMA DEFINED THE TERM "PIECE OF WORK."
IN MY NEW BUSINESS, YOU NEVER KNEW WHEN YOU MIGHT NEED ONE OF THOSE.

CON MAN, FELON, BATTERER, FREQUENT ISSUER OF THREATS OF VIOLENCE.
TOOK YOU LONG ENOUGH.
I'M NOT WHO YOU THINK. D.O.D. DOESN'T KNOW YOU.
THAT IS, ASSUMING THEY EVER DID KNOW YOU.

I'D RUN INTO HIM IN THE BUSINESS CENTER OF THE HOTEL TAJIKISTAN, MEDIA NERVE CENTER DURING THE FALL 2001 U.S. INVASION OF AFGHANISTAN. HE CLAIMED TO BE A SPECIAL FORCES ADVISOR TO THE NORTHERN ALLIANCE. BUT WHEN I CHECKED WITH D.O.D., THEY "DKED" HIM—DENIED HAVING ANY AFFILIATION WHATSOEVER
DON'T LOOK AT THESE FILES UNLESS YOU'VE GOT THE BALLS.

IDEMA SOON WENT FULL-BORE COLONEL KURTZ. HE AND TWO BUDDIES RAN A FREELANCE TORTURE OPERATION CALLED "TASK FORCE SABER 7" OUT OF A CELLAR IN KABUL. THEY KIDNAPPED RANDOM AFGHANS OFF THE STREET AND ASKED THEM WHERE OSAMA BIN LADEN (REWARD: $25 MILLION) WAS UNTIL THEY DIED. IN 2004, AFGHAN COPS FOUND EIGHT DUDES HANGING UPSIDE DOWN FROM CHAINS, BLOOD FROM KNIFE SLASHES DRIPPING INTO BUCKETS.
THEY SENTENCED HIM TO TEN YEARS IN PRISON—A DEATH SENTENCE. THING IS, AFGHAN PRISON GUARDS DON'T GET PAID MUCH... SOMETIMES NOTHING AT ALL.
56

THIS TURD WOULD BE USEFUL.
DON'T FUCK WITH ME. YOU HAVE NO IDEA WHO I'M CONNECTED WITH.
CUT THE CRAP, IDEMA. IF I WANTED TO FUCK WITH YOU, NO ONE WOULD CARE. BUT I'M NOT HERE TO FUCK WITH YOU. I'M HERE TO GET YOU OUT OF PRISON —CHECK!— AND MAKE YOU RICH.
AND YOU RICHER.
MUCH RICHER.

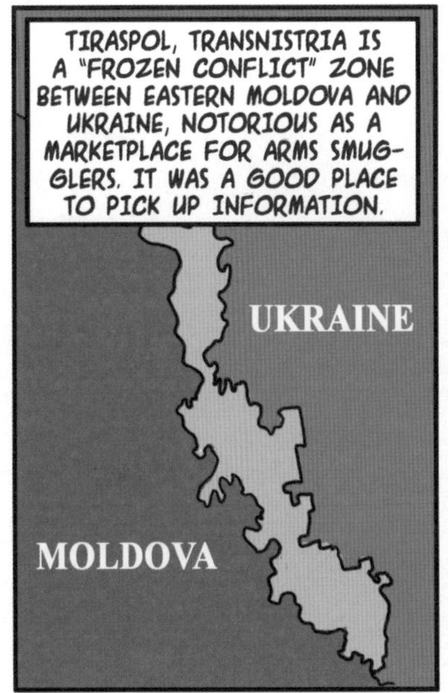

Tolkuchka Bazaar outside Ashkhabat, Turkmenistan

M39 highway, southwest Kazakhstan near the Cosmodrome space facility

58

TARGET IS NO LONGER MOVING!

ANOTHER VEHICLE HAS PULLED IN FRONT OF IT.
EITHER A TRUCK OR A BUS.

NICE WORK, LIEUTENANT. KEEP A LOCK AND LET ME KNOW IF THERE SEEMS TO BE A TRANSFER.

59

THEY'RE MOVING AGAIN?
YES, SIR.

"DEFINITELY
NO TRANSFER."
60

DID I KNOW WHAT I WAS DOING?
OF COURSE NOT.

EVERYONE SAYS THEY KNOW WHAT THEY'RE DOING.
LIARS!

WE'RE ALL JUST BLUNDERING AROUND.

BULLSHITTING OUR WAY THROUGH LIFE.

I WASN'T SOME CRIMINAL MASTERMIND.
I WASN'T —I'M NOT— A GENIUS.

INTELLIGENCE IS RELATIVE.

I'M NOT SMART.
EVERYONE ELSE IS SO GODDAMN STUPID.

SPEAKING OF STUPID: WESTERN FOREIGN POLICYMAKERS SPEND EVERY WAKING SECOND PROMOTING CAPITALISM. BUT NOT FOR PEOPLE. FOR CORPORATIONS. THEY ALWAYS FORGET THE INDIVIDUALS. DON'T THEY GET IT? THE PROFIT INCENTIVE APPLIES TO US TOO.
GORBACHEV SAYS USSR IS FINISHED. NUCLEAR PROGRAM IS FINISHED. GO HOME.
WITH NO MONEY?
WHAT ARE WE SUPPOSED TO DO? JUST DIE?

Semipalatinsk-21 Test Site atomic testing facility, aka "The Polygon," northeastern Kazakh Soviet Socialist Republic, USSR, 1989

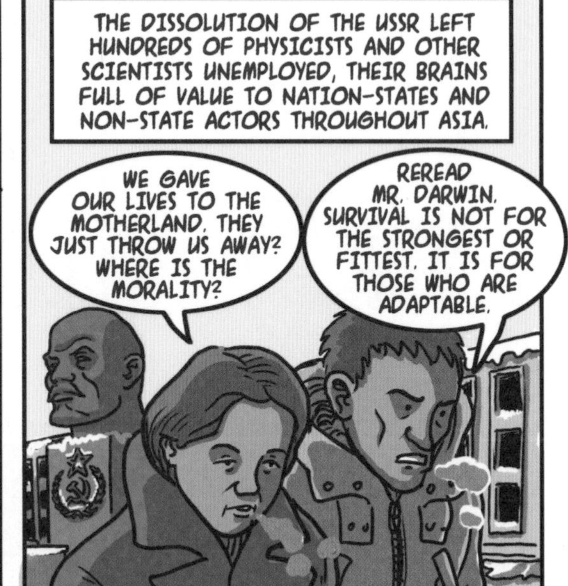

THE DISSOLUTION OF THE USSR LEFT HUNDREDS OF PHYSICISTS AND OTHER SCIENTISTS UNEMPLOYED, THEIR BRAINS FULL OF VALUE TO NATION-STATES AND NON-STATE ACTORS THROUGHOUT ASIA.
WE GAVE OUR LIVES TO THE MOTHERLAND. THEY JUST THROW US AWAY? WHERE IS THE MORALITY?
REREAD MR. DARWIN. SURVIVAL IS NOT FOR THE STRONGEST OR FITTEST. IT IS FOR THOSE WHO ARE ADAPTABLE.

MOST OF THE DISPOSSESSED RESIGNED THEMSELVES TO THE DOWNWARD MOBILITY OF MIDDLE AGE IN AN OUTPOST OF A COLLAPSING EMPIRE.

OTHERS DID NOT.
THERE IS TALK OF REPATRIATION. AT PRESENT, HOWEVER, KAZAKHSTAN IS LEFT WITH 1,150 STRATEGIC NUCLEAR WARHEADS.
UNDER YOUR SAFEKEEPING.
CORRECT.

Juma Namangani and Tohir Yuldashev, leaders of the Islamic Movement of Uzbekistan (IMU), Taliban-trained insurgent group based in Tajikistan and Kyrgyzstan

YOUR PRICE IS HIGH.
WHAT I OFFER IS A GAME CHANGER.

FIVE YEARS LATER, THE INTERNATIONAL COMMUNITY WAS STILL SMUGLY GLOATING OVER HOW DEFTLY IT HAD HANDLED THE DEFEAT OF COMMUNISM.
WE ARE PLEASED TO ANNOUNCE THE REPATRIATION OF ALL 1,140 WEAPONS.
TO A PEACEFUL, NUCLEAR—FREE KAZAKHSTAN!

Joint announcement between Kazakh President Nursultan Nazarbayev and International Atomic Energy Agency, Almaty, Kazakhstan

AS A JOURNALIST, I HAD ALWAYS BEEN IN THE WAR BUSINESS.
rovince, Yemen
PHOSPHORUS-BASED WEAPONS MARK A BRUTAL ESCALATION OF THE ASSAULT ON THE HOUTHI REBELS, WHO ARE EMBEDDED WITH THE CIVILIAN POPULATION HERE.
THESE MARKINGS SEEM TO BELIE AMERICAN DENIALS OF INVOLVEMENT.
ON TV
MARK SCRIBNER, SENIOR CORRESPONDENT/ANALYS
Scribner wins second Pulitzer ... Watch Scribner exclusively on C
CNN

NOW I WAS IN THE BUSINESS OF WAR.
AND BUSINESS WAS GOOD.
GIVEN MARK'S IMPRESSIVE RATINGS, WE'RE LOOKING FOR A 350% INCREASE.
BUT WE CAN'T COMMIT TO MORE THAN ANOTHER YEAR.
THAT'S ACCEPTABLE.
WE'LL DISCUSS IT ON AN ENCRYPTED LINE.

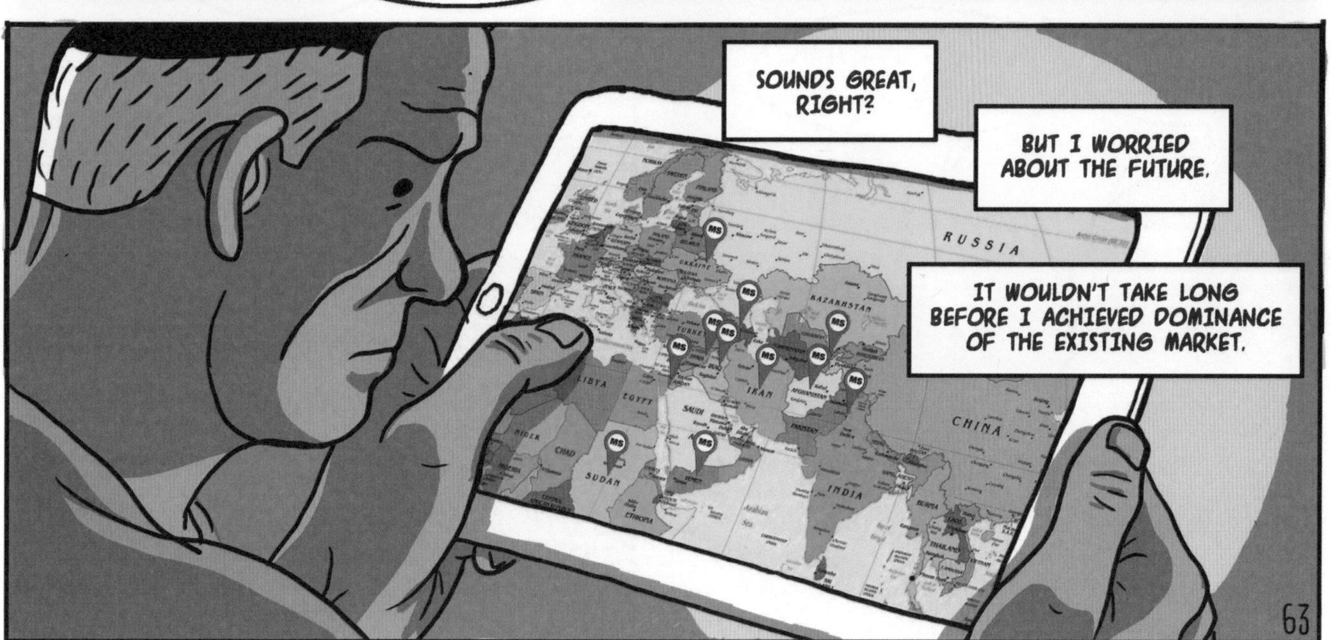
SOUNDS GREAT, RIGHT?
BUT I WORRIED ABOUT THE FUTURE.
IT WOULDN'T TAKE LONG BEFORE I ACHIEVED DOMINANCE OF THE EXISTING MARKET.
RUSSIA
CHINA
INDIA
63

PARTICULARLY IN THE CAUCASUS AND CENTRAL/SOUTH ASIAN SECTORS, CURRENT TRENDS ARE UNFAVORABLE TO OUR MUTUAL CONCERNS.
WHEN YOU DOMINATE, YOU HURT YOUR COMPETITORS' BOTTOM LINES.
I DON'T LIKE THE MARK SCRIBNER TREND.
POWERFUL INTERESTS WERE WATCHING ME WITH GREAT UNEASE.

WE UNDERSTAND THAT SOMETHING... UNORTHODOX... MAY BE CALLED FOR.
WE HAVE EXPERIENCE WITH THIS SORT OF PROBLEM.

DOMINANCE MAKES YOU A TARGET. IN A LINE OF WORK IN WHICH KILLING IS KEY, DOMINANCE IS DANGEROUS.
A BUSINESSMAN WHO TRIES TO CORNER A MARKET IS A PIG.

A PIG IS STUPID. I WASN'T STUPID. I SHARED. SHARING DECONCENTRATES RISK.
YOU CAN SOURCE THESE? WHERE?
NOT WHERE.
HOW.
I GIVE YOU THE TECH GRATIS. YOU MANUFACTURE AND SELL UP TO 500 A YEAR. NOT TOO MANY OR THE DOD WILL GO APESHIT.
ALL I ASK FOR MYSELF IS 75; I COVER FREIGHT.

NO ISIS, NO HEZBOLLAH.
FUCK ISIS—DEADBEATS. BUT HEZBOLLAH IS A MAJOR CLIENT.
SHALL WE SAY ONE DOZEN, ONLY HALF ARMED?
64

LIKE ANY GOOD BUSINESSPERSON, HOWEVER, I CRAVED EXPANSION. HOW DO YOU GROW WITHOUT PUSHING OUT POTENTIAL RIVALS AND TURNING COMPETITORS INTO MORTAL ENEMIES?
BY EXPANDING THE ENTIRE MARKET.
China
Laos
Thailand
Vietnam
Cambodia
Paracel islands
Spratly islands
Philippines
Malaysia
Malaysia
THE CENTRAL POLITBURO IS DEEPLY CONCERNED ABOUT AMERICAN PROVOCATIONS WITHIN OUR SPHERE OF INFLUENCE.
YOU NEED PARITY.
DEBORAH'S CYBER DIVISION HAS DEVELOPED NON-TRACEABLE VIRUSES FOR USAF NAVIGATION SYSTEMS.

OBVIOUSLY, THAT MEANT MORE WARS.
BREAKING NEWS
SUDAN PEACE DEAL
LIVE
CNN
THE PEOPLE OF SOUTH SUDAN ARE HOPEFUL THAT PEACE IS FINALLY AT HAND IN THEIR WAR-TORN COUNTRY.
WE'LL SEE.

IT MEANT THOSE WARS HAD TO GET BIGGER.

DRDO

BOOOM!

Western command center, Pakistani-Indian Line of Control, Kashmir province
WHAT THE HELL JUST HAPPENED?
65

I KNEW HOW TO MAKE MORE WARS.
IT ISN'T US, MR. PRESIDENT. WE'RE WITH YOU 100%.
INDEPENDENT News Business Sports Tech Culture
News > World > Americas
FARC maoist front reconstituted stronger than ever thanks to U.S. arms smuggled via Venezuela.
John Doe | 12:34 GMT | 375 Comments
IT'S EITHER YOU OR THE FUCKING VENEZUELANS.
President Juan Manuel Santos meets with US Embassy/CIA liaisons

THE QUESTION WAS, HOW TO MAKE THE WARS WE STARTED BIGGER, BETTER, MORE PROFITABLE AND MORE NEWSWORTHY?
FARC? BEEN THERE, DONE THAT. SORRY, MARK.
CNN
ONE ANSWER WAS: MORE WEAPONS. BIGGER WEAPONS.

LOTS OF JOURNALISTS HAD TAKEN SECOND JOBS TO GET BY.
I HAVE A BLOG.
REALLY INTERESTING STUFF.
YOU CAN CHECK IT OUT AT WWW.H-A-—
UH-HUH. I'M UP HERE ON THE RIGHT.

SO DID I. I BECAME AN ARMS DEALER.
NEAT.
World Arms Trade Magazine
Micro - Drones
The next big small thing
66

MY YEARS AS A JOURNALIST BROUGHT ME INTO CONTACT WITH EVERYONE EVERYWHERE. MY ROLODEX WAS NO LONGER WORTH ANYTHING IN THE WORLD OF JOURNALISM.

LAST NIGHT, THE CHEMICAL PLANT YOU TOLD ME ABOUT.
YOUR BROTHER SAW IT WITH HIS OWN EYES?
CAN I HAVE HIS NUMBER?
BUT THE DEVIL MAKES WORK FOR IDLE HANDS—WHEN THOSE HANDS ARE HIGHLY TRAINED. MY WORK TURNED OUT TO HAVE BEEN THE IDEAL APPRENTICESHIP FOR A FUTURE MERCHANT OF DEATH.

I KNEW ALL THE PLAYERS: THE WARLORDS, THE ASPIRING TYRANTS, THE "LEGITIMATE" NATION-STATE POLITICIANS OUT FOR PERSONAL AND POLITICAL GAIN, ALL WILLING TO KILL TO GET WHAT THEY WANTED.
AL SHABAB? WE DO NOT KNOW THEM.

DRONES, MY MAN.
DRONES ARE THE FUTURE.

OF COURSE I KNEW THE SUPPLIERS. IN MY CIRCLES, THEY WERE HARD TO AVOID.
ADVANCE SALES OF THE F-76 THUNDERBOLT FIGHTER SET US UP NICELY FOR Q4.
WHAT ABOUT DEFICIT HAWKS CRITICS IN THE SENATE?

YOU'RE ASKING A LOT.
I'M PAYING A LOT.

NEVER MIND BANK REFORM—FINANCIERS ARE ALWAYS HAPPY TO TAKE YOUR MONEY.
THIS WILL BE A NUMBERED ACCOUNT.
I REQUIRE SUBSTANTIAL SUMS OF CASH TRANSMITTED CONFIDENTIALLY, WITHOUT TRACE.
OF COURSE. THERE WILL BE NO ELECTRONIC OR TELEPHONIC COMMUNICA-TIONS.
CASH ONLY. NO WIRES. SOME RECIPIENTS HAVE ISSUES WITH TRADE SANCTIONS.
NO PROBLEM.

FINDING THE RIGHT MIDDLEMEN WAS TRICKY. YOU CAN'T EXPAND WITHOUT WORKING WITH SOME UNTRUSTWORTHY CHARACTERS. PROPER MANAGEMENT IS KEY.

I WILL—
SHUT UP.
YOU WILL SHUT UP.
AND I WILL PAY YOU.
AND EVERYONE WILL BE HAPPY.
AND YOU WILL NEVER EVER TALK.

I'D ALWAYS HAD AN INSTINCT FOR FIXERS.
I FEEL RESPONSIBLE FOR WHAT HAPPENED TO JOVID. YOUR BROTHER WAS A GOOD MAN. ALWAYS GOOD AT THE FRONT.
HE LOVED YOU, MR. MARK. WHICH IS WHY I BRING YOU CONTACT WITH MY FATHER.

THE FORMER PHYSICIST.
PLEASE ASK HIM, DOES HE HAVE ACCESS TO EXPLODING FOIL INITIATORS?
PETN?
HEXANITROSTILBENE?

CLIENTS? THEY WERE THE EASIEST PIECE OF THE PUZZLE.
AND WHO WILL BE THE RECIPIENTS OF THE RELEVANT ITEMS?
YOU CAN PROBABLY GUESS THAT.
I'D LIKE TO HEAR IT DIRECTLY.
NOTHING IN THE MIDDLE EAST IS EVER DIRECT, MR. SCRIBNER.
68

I WAS A PERFECTIONIST.

WHEN I NEEDED AN ASSHOLE, I NEEDED A PERFECT ASSHOLE.
AS IDEMA WAS.

PHONE
Harare, Zimbabwe

COME WITH ME.

I NEED YOU TO CLEAR SPACE ON THE PRESIDENT'S CALENDAR. MY FRIEND NEEDS TO MEET WITH HIM.
I CAN'T DO THAT.

WRONG ANSWER.
POW!
69
LET'S TRY AGAIN: HOW DOES THE PRESIDENT'S SCHEDULE LOOK NOW?
BETTER. OPEN. VERY OPEN!
THE RIGHT PERSONAL ASSISTANT MAKES ALL THE DIFFERENCE.

ERBIL IS NEXT.
HOLD ON, I HAVE ANOTHER CALL—
MARGREET.
MARK! SO GOOD TO HEAR YOUR VOICE.

SmartNews
I KNOW YOU'RE BUSY SO I'LL CUT TO THE CHASE.
HOW WOULD YOU FEEL ABOUT BEING THE OLDEST PERSON IN THE ROOM?
ALSO THE PAY IS SHIT, THE HOURS ARE LONG AND YOU DON'T GET AN OFFICE. BUT WE'RE DOING GOOD WORK.
QUITE THE SALES PITCH!

YOU DON'T NEED MONEY, MARK. BUT WE NEED YOU.
YOUR EXPERIENCE.
YOUR GUTS.
YOUR JOURNALISTIC ETHICS.

WE'RE UP FOR A THIRD ROUND OF FUNDING AND WE'D LOVE TO HAVE YOU ABOARD.
I'D LOVE TO. BUT—

MEIKLES HOTEL
Harare
Jendayi
Your room attendant
I have taken special pride in preparing this room for you.
I hope you find everything satisfactory.
Have a pleasant day!
RESERVE BANK OF ZIMBABWE
ONE HUNDRED TRILLION
I'M RETIRING.

ONCE I COMMITTED TO A COURSE OF ACTION, I WENT ALL IN. NO HALF-MEASURES.
WHAT EXACTLY CAN YOU PROVIDE?
ANYTHING YOU WANT, I CAN GET.

YOU MIGHT BE SURPRISED AT WHAT I WANT.
YOU MIGHT BE SURPRISED AT HOW HARD IT IS TO SURPRISE ME.

President Robert Gabriel Mugabe of Zimbabwe

ANY ASSHOLE COULD SHILL RUSTY AK-47s AND DUD RPGs TO INSURGENTS. I WAS DETERMINED TO BECOME A FULL-SERVICE OPERATION. I'D OFFER *EVERYTHING*.
REALLY?
REALLY.
IF YOU HAVE THE MONEY.

Tarkhan Gaziyev, Emir of the South-Western sector of Vilayat Nokhchicho, Caucasus Emirate

CHALLENGE ONE: KEEPING MY ENEMIES HAPPY.
YOUR MARKET SHARE KEEPS GROWING.
AS DOES YOUR MARKET CAPITALIZATION, YES?

CHALLENGE TWO:

HANDLING CASH.

THREE IF YOU COUNTED MORALS. FORTUNATELY, THOSE WERE EASILY DISPOSED OF.
THE TWO BALD GUYS ARE FSB?
RUSSIA DOESN'T LIKE THE COMPETITION. THEY'VE BEEN FOLLOWING ME.
Pearl-Continental

WE WILL CHOP THEM INTO PIECES AND FEED THEM TO THE DOGS.
THAT WORKS.

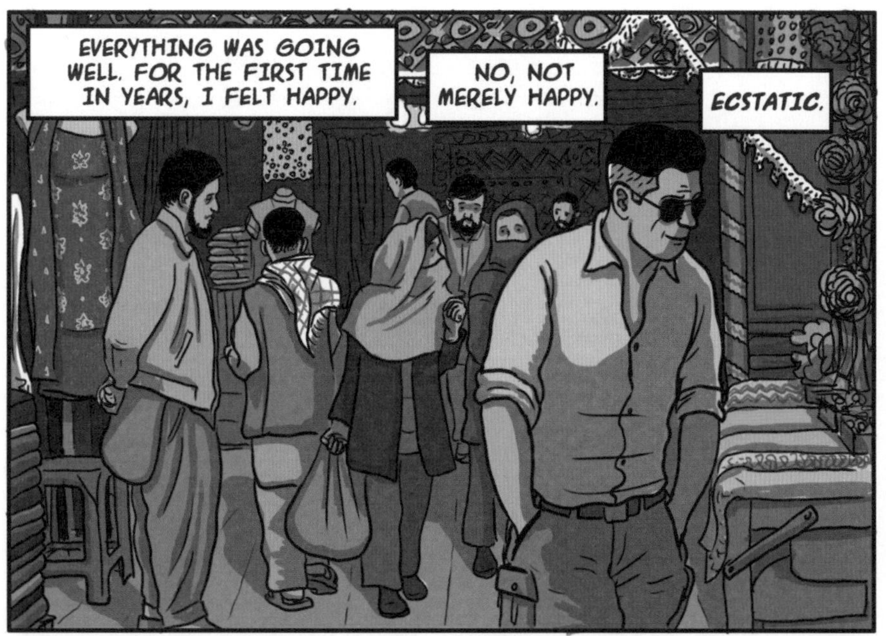
EVERYTHING WAS GOING WELL. FOR THE FIRST TIME IN YEARS, I FELT HAPPY.
NO, NOT MERELY HAPPY.
ECSTATIC.

EVER WATCHED A CAT PLAY WITH A MOUSE?

99.99% OF THE TIME, A HOUSECAT LIES AROUND, BORED OUT OF ITS MIND.

BUT A MOUSE CHANGES EVERYTHING.

CATCHING MICE IS WHY THAT CAT WAS PUT HERE ON EARTH.
THAT CAT HAS NEVER BEEN MORE ALIVE.
MOST PEOPLE FIND IT REVOLTING.

NOT ME.
I THINK IT'S BEAUTIFUL TO WATCH.
73

I WAS LIKE THAT CAT.
I WAS AS ALIVE AS A CAT LIKE THAT.

MAYBE THAT'S WHY MY INSTINCTS WERE SHARP.
OverSea Tourist & Travel Agency
Kabul, Afghanistan

Philadelphia
BREAKING NEWS
RUSSIA PROTESTS 2 MISSING EMBASSY STAFFERS IN PAKISTAN

I NEED A ONE-WAY ON TONIGHT'S 8 O'CLOCK PLANE TO ZARANJ.
THERE IS NO FLIGHT TO ZARANJ TONIGHT.
PARIS

EVERY THURSDAY ONLY, BUT IT IS SOLD OUT.
SOLD OUT? NOT A PROBLEM.

I AM PREPARED TO—

SHE WAS AN APPARITION.

AIR FRANCE

OverSea Tourist & Travel Agency
airblue
SHAHEEN AIR
express

Afsana
788-230-212

BMA
Bank-e-Millie Afghan

WHAT WAS I SAYING AGAIN?

OH, RIGHT, INSTINCTS.

HOW DID YOU GET MY NUMBER?

I WAS HAVING A GOOD TIME. BUT I WASN'T AN IDIOT.

KILLED? HOW?
I AM SO HAPPY TONIGHT. CAN WE TALK ABOUT THAT ANOTHER TIME?

I WAS STEPPING ON A LOT OF TOES, SO IT WAS ONLY A MATTER OF TIME BEFORE SOMEONE WHO MATTERED CAUGHT ON.

Military Counterintelligence Directorate, Federal Security Service of the Russian Federation, Lubyanka Square, Moscow, Russia
PLEASE SUMMARIZE, AGENT KUZNETSOV.
OF COURSE, MR. DIRECTOR.
AS YOU ALL KNOW, OUR COLLEAGUES IN THE DIRECTORATE FOR TERRORISM AND POLITICAL EXTREMISM CONTROL HAVE BELIEVED THAT CERTAIN CONFLICTS HAVE BEEN ESCALATED AND/OR PROVOKED EXTERNALLY BY A NON-STATE ACTOR.

INITIALLY THEY SUSPECTED SELF-RADICALIZATION VIA THE INTERNET.
EITHER ISIS OR SOME OTHER VIRAL NON-HIERARCHICAL MOVEMENT, MOST LIKELY ISLAMIST GIVEN THE LOCATIONS.

THANKS TO EXCELLENT COOPERATION FROM THE FEDERAL AGENCY OF GOVERNMENT COMMUNICATIONS AND INFORMATION, HOWEVER, WE NOW BELIEVE NEITHER A STATE NOR A NON-STATE ENTITY IS RESPONSIBLE.
Абд-Раббу Мансур Хади
США
Саудовская Аравия
Кувейт
Пакистан
Иран
КНДР
Ансарулла
Хезболла
Эритрея

INTERCEPTS POINT TO A HIGHLY-RESPECTED AMERICAN JOURNALIST.

THIS INDIVIDUAL STARTS A WAR, TYPICALLY BY HACKING SOCIAL MEDIA. HE CHOOSES ZONES WHERE MANY WEAPONS ARE ALREADY ON SITE, SO HIS STAGED CONFLICTS ESCALATE QUICKLY.

THEN HE SELLS MORE, BETTER, WEAPONS TO BOTH SIDES.
AT EVEN LEVELS, SO THE SLAUGHTER CONTINUES.
BLYAD!
("MOTHERFUCKER!")

WE'VE TOLD THE AMERICANS. BUT THEY THINK WE'RE MAKING THIS SHIT UP TO COVER UP OUR OWN INCREASED ARMS SALES.
THIS ASSHOLE IS GOOD FOR BUSINESS.

BUT HE'S ALSO ESCALATING TENSIONS, AND NOT JUST BETWEEN US AND THE U.S.
IF HE KEEPS THIS UP, THERE WON'T BE A WORLD LEFT TO SELL WEAPONS TO.

СДЕЛАЙ ЭТО
("DO IT.")

I DON'T CARE WHAT ANYONE THINKS. I AM MY OWN PERSON.

THAT'S NOT EASY HERE.
IT'S THE ONLY WAY TO LIVE.

WE'VE BOTH LOST SO MANY PEOPLE.
IF TRAGEDY IS A STRANGER TO YOU, I CAN BE YOUR FRIEND. BUT YOU CAN'T REALLY KNOW ME. YOU CANNOT TRULY LOVE ME NOR I YOU.
WHEN I GIVE MYSELF I GIVE MYSELF COMPLETELY. I WILL DO ANYTHING FOR YOU. SO YOU MUST PROMISE ME YOU WILL BE THE SAME FOR ME.

ACTUALLY... YOU DO NOT NEED TO PROMISE ME ANYTHING.

I SEE IT IN YOUR EYES.
78

KHWAJA RAWASH
apartment complex

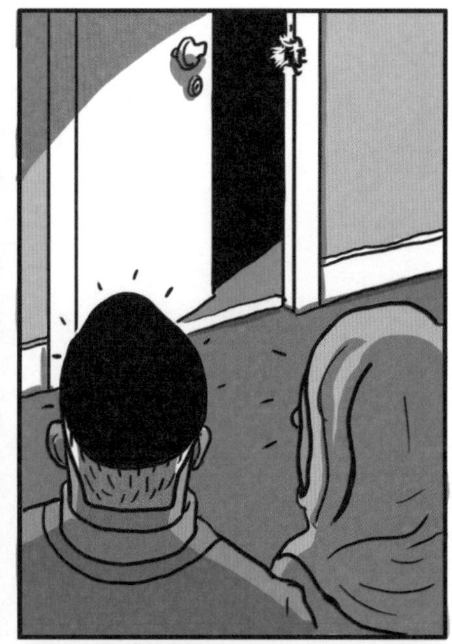

STAY HERE. IF YOU HEAR NOISE, RUN.

CLICK!

Mark Scribner
Dispatches from Afghanistan
The New Media PARADOX
Mark Scribner
The Future of War Correspondency
Mark Scribner
Mark Scribner
ASSIGNMENT NAMIBIA
Secrets and lies of war journalism
Unembedded in Iraq
Mark Scribner

WHOEVER IT WAS IS GONE.
DOESN'T LOOK LIKE THEY HAD TIME TO TAKE MUCH.
THANK GOD!

BUT HE PLANTED THESE TO MAKE YOU LOOK LIKE SOMEONE WITH NO TASTE.
Mark Scribner
ASSIGNMENT NAMIBIA

I'LL CALL SOMEONE TO FIX THE DOOR. I CAN ALSO HAVE SOMEONE DISCREET WATCH OUTSIDE.
MARK—

MARK, I KNEW WHO YOU WERE THE SECOND YOU WALKED INTO THE TRAVEL AGENCY.

THAT'S NOT SURPRISING. I'M ON TV.
THAT'S NOT WHAT I MEAN.

I MEAN, I KNEW YOU.
ABOUT YOU.
MORE THAN THAT: I KNEW *YOU.*

MEANWHILE, IN WASHINGTON...
J. Edgar Hoover FBI Building

WHAT DO YOU MAKE OF THIS?
CLASSIC RUSSIAN FSB DISINFOR-MATION.
CONFIDENTIAL
TV JOURNALIST TURNS WARLORD? RIDICULOUS.

THEY THINK THE RUSSIANS ARE FULL OF SHIT, MARK.
THEY HAVE NOTHING ON YOU.
EVEN THE FISA COURT WON'T ISSUE A WARRANT.

THANK YOU, LORI.
81

KABUL SERENA
HOTEL

I WILL CHECK THIS FOR YOU, SIR.
THAN—

CNN GIVE YOU THAT?

TECHNICALLY I'M FREELANCE. PICKED IT UP AT THE JAMRUD BAZAAR ALONG WITH A PAIR OF AKs.
STILL WORKING FOR THAT DEAD-TREES OUTFIT, FAHIM?
YEAH, THE *TIMES*. VERY OLD-SCHOOL. LIKE, THEY DON'T BELIEVE IN ARMING THEIR REPORTERS.
WHAT THE HELL ARE YOU *DOING*, SCRIBNER?

NOT GETTING KILLED. YOU SHOULD TRY IT.
YOU MIGHT ALSO TRY RESPECT FOR YOUR BETTERS.
ALL THE PEABODYS IN THE WORLD CAN'T MAKE WHAT YOU'RE DOING OK.
YEAH?

AND WHAT EXACTLY AM I *DOING* ?!?

I ADMIRED YOU WHEN YOU WERE DOWN AND OUT, MAN.
YOU WERE REAL.
NOW— WHAT THE FUCK?
83

FAHIM HAD A POINT.

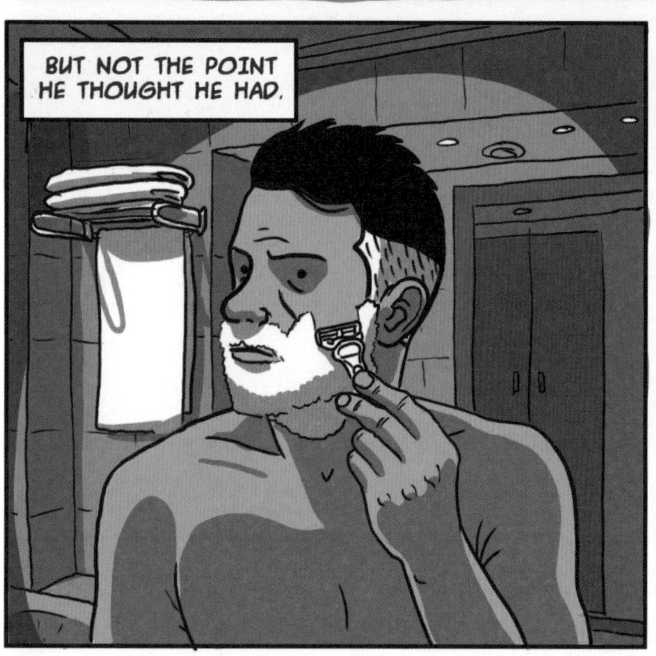
BUT NOT THE POINT HE THOUGHT HE HAD.

WHAT I WAS DOING WAS MORE THAN OK — OK FOR ME.
WHAT IT WAS NOT WAS SMART.

IN AN OSSIFIED SECTOR LIKE JOURNALISM, ESPECIALLY IN CONFLICT REPORTING, YOU CAN'T GET AHEAD WITHOUT BEING DISRUPTIVE.
TODAY
SPECIAL GUEST: MARK SCRIBNER
TODAY

BUT THE ACTUAL *CONFLICTS* WERE ANYTHING BUT STUCK.
WAR IS INSTABILITY. IT IS DISRUPTION.
WHEN YOU DISRUPT THAT SECTOR, ESPECIALLY AS SEVERELY AS I HAD, YOU'RE PLAYING WITH FIRE.
AIRPORT.
TAXI

I WAS FLYING HIGH.
044025299. CHESHIRE. GATO.
BALANCE, PLEASE.

€112,050,113.58
OUR ASSOCIATES HAVE OPENED A BITCOIN ACCOUNT FOR YOU AS REQUESTED.
AND THE OTHER MATTER?
CURRENT BALANCE IS 250,000 BITCOINS.

IT WAS TIME TO START BRINGING MYSELF IN FOR A SOFT LANDING.
KABUL AIRPORT

I WOULD WIND DOWN MY OPERATIONS.

SOME MATTERS SHOULD BE HANDED OVER TO MY PARTNERS. OTHERS, I SHOULD JUST QUIT.

WE WILL BE LEAVING FOR CHAGHCHARAN IN A FEW MINUTES.
85

ACTUALLY, THIS IS THE SAFEST AIRPLANE ON EARTH.
YOU THINK SOME TERRORIST IS GOING TO TRY ANYTHING HERE?

YOU ARE A FAILURE!
USELESS!

WOULD SHE— ?

YOU'RE SUCH A LOSE—

NO. IT WON'T BE LIKE THAT.
86

ALL I GOTTA DO IS GET RID OF MY LOOSE ENDS.

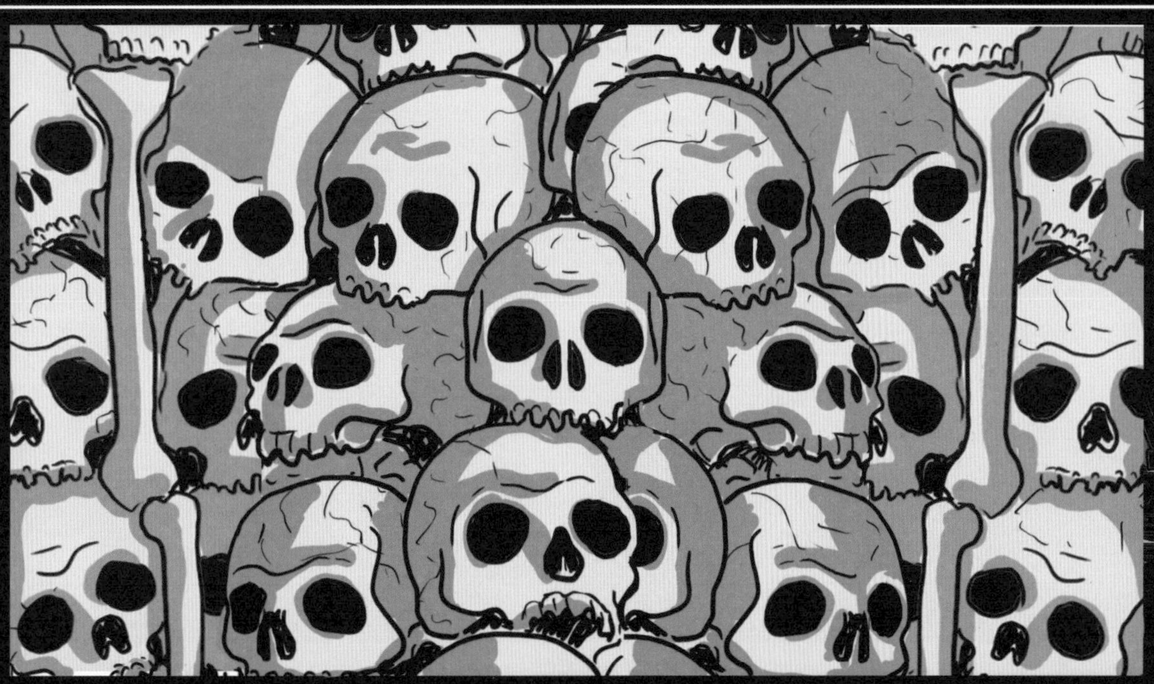

Chaghcharan, Afghanistan

WE'RE RUNNING LOW ON RPG WARHEADS. SHEIKH FAZEL IS ASKING WHEN WE CAN EXPECT THE NEXT SHIPMENT.
I AM SORRY, ALAUDDIN. I'M WINDING DOWN MY BUSINESS.

TELL THE SHEIKH EVERYTHING WILL BE OK. CONTACT INFORMATION FOR MY GOOD FRIEND IN TASHKENT.
A GOOD FRIEND.

SAME QUALITY PRODUCT.
SAME PRICE.
NO DELAY IN SHIPMENT.

Office of Mustafa Sayid Qadir, Minister of Peshmerga Affairs of the Kurdistan Regional Government, Arbil, Iraq
WE WILL MISS YOU, MR. SCRIBNER. YOUR SERVICE TO THE KURDISH STRUGGLE WILL NOT BE FORGOTTEN.

Wong's Chinese Cuisine
Broadway
Free delivery
Upper West Side of Manhattan

SO WHAT'S THIS YOU WANTED TO TELL ME ABOUT SCRIBNER?
I DON'T FEEL AWESOME. I GOTTA GO HOME. I'LL TELL YOU NEXT TIME.

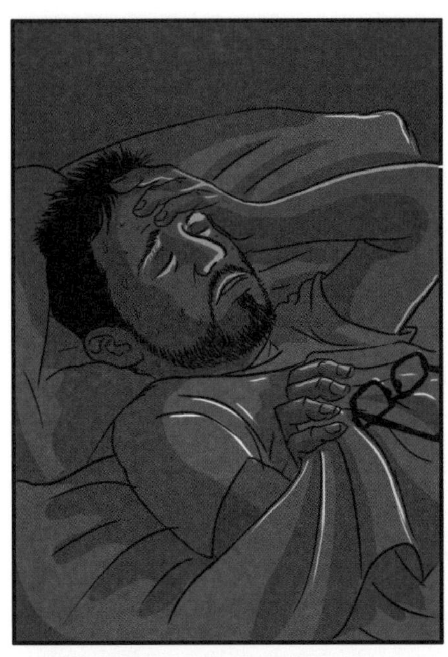

Fahim Abed, Reporter for the Times, is dead at
by LARRY CALLAHAN
Fahim Abed

FAHIM WAS A JOURNALIST'S JOURNALIST. HE ONLY CARED ABOUT THE TRUTH. HE DIDN'T CARE WHAT THE TRUTH WAS.

FUNERAL HOME

THE SECOND HALF OF THE MONEY IS IN YOUR ACCOUNT.

IT WASN'T PERSONAL, FAHIM. YOU WERE A LOOSE END.

WHAT? NO.
OF COURSE I DIDN'T QUIT.
I STREAMLINED.

I DUMPED THE PENNY-ANTE SHIT I DIDN'T HAVE TIME FOR.

I ADMIT, I DID GET DISTRACTED BY SOME OF THE POSSIBILITIES OFFERED BY EMERGING TECHNOLOGIES.
SAN FRANCISCO TECH CONFERENCE
TECH City
5G

OUR SPEECH SYNTHESIS SERVICE PULLS TOGETHER AN ARCHIVE OF YOUR SUBJECT'S PUBLICLY AVAILABLE VOICE RECORDINGS IN ORDER TO CREATE A DATABASE OF COMMONLY USED SYLLABLES AND WORDS.
TTS
Text To Speech
one step ahead in communication
Palo Alto CA

OUR TEXT-TO-SPEECH (TTS) SYSTEM CONVERTS YOUR TEXT INTO THEIR SPEECH.
WE CAN ALSO RENDER SYMBOLIC LINGUISTIC REPRESENTATIONS LIKE PHONETIC TRANSCRIPTIONS INTO SPEECH...
... AND MATCH IT WITH TONAL CHANGES SIGNIFYING EMOTIONS LIKE HAPPINESS AND SADNESS AND SARCASM AND WHATEVER SO THE FACIAL EXPRESSIONS MATCH UP.

WE CAN CREATE A VIDEO THAT MAKES IT LOOK LIKE HE SAID ANYTHING WE WANT!

BANANA BATSHIT BUBBLEGUM BOOHOO!
93

SOME PEOPLE CALLED IT "DEEP FAKE."
NO SHIT!

MY OLD COLLEAGUES? THEY DIDN'T HAVE A CLUE ABOUT HOW THE NEW WORLD WORKS.

WHICH WAS WHY THEY WERE ALL BEING LAID OFF.

STILL, I ADMIRED THEM. JUST BECAUSE THEY WEREN'T WILLING TO PROSTITUTE THE ETHICS THEY CAME OF AGE WITH DIDN'T MEAN I DISLIKED THEM.
BLOODBATH!
Once-promising "New Media" platforms lay off hundreds of young journalists
By Ben Haberman
Margreet van den Basten, co-founder of SmartNews

THEY GOT SCREWED.

THE DIFFERENCE BETWEEN ME AND THEM WAS THAT I COULDN'T LIVE WITH IT.
THANKS FOR THE RIDE.
SURE...

SOMETHING FROM MARK.

500 EURO
Quit driving
and retire
already

WHAT THE HELL?

Saldo EUR
valuta
07-02
+763,74
-73,50
02 4077 07-02
-185,20
624 9960 07-02
-80,00
7845 7744 09-02
+1.000.000,00
1411 3825 09-02
1.000.425,04
Nieuw saldo EUR

95

THIS $10 MILLION DONATION IS YOURS BASED ON TWO CONDITIONS.

FIRST, YOUR BENEFACTOR WISHES TO REMAIN ANONYMOUS. IF YOU SO MUCH AS SPECULATE PUBLICLY ABOUT ITS ORIGINS THE OFFER IS NULL AND THE MONEY MUST BE RETURNED.
SECOND, YOU MUST DEDICATE YOURSELF FULL-TIME TO BUILDING A NEW PLATFORM FOR INDEPENDENT ADVOCACY JOURNALISM AND INVESTIGATIVE REPORTING.
AS FOR THE THIRD CONDITION, THIS IS A QUOTE: "QUIT THE TIMES. NO MORE FUCKING CORPORATE SHILLS."

IT WAS TIME TO MEET THE PARENTS.

LIKE MANY OTHER AFGHANS, AFSANA'S FAMILY FLED AFGHANISTAN AND SCATTERED ACROSS ASIA FROM THE AFTERMATH OF THE DIASPORA THAT FOLLOWED THE SOVIET AND POST-SOVIET CIVIL WARS OF THE 1980s AND 1990s.
ISLAMABAD INTERNATIONAL AIRPORT

GILGIT
NORTHERN AREAS

THEY LIVED UP THE HIGH-ALTITUDE KARAKORAM HIGHWAY IN A BRANCH OF THE HIMALAYAS THAT WAS THE INSPIRATION FOR THE MYTH OF SHANGRI-LA.

THE KARAKORAM HIGHWAY CONNECTS ISLAMABAD, PAKISTAN TO KASHGAR, CHINA VIA PAKISTANI KASHMIR (THE NORTHERN AREAS).

THIS WAS THE SECTION OF DISPUTED KASHMIR ADMINISTERED BY PAKISTAN AFTER THE PARTITION OF INDIA AND A TRIO OF WARS.

96

IT WAS RUGGED, BEAUTIFUL, TIMELESS.

<Afsani is an honorable girl.>
<I would kill anyone who dishonored her. Including myself.>

<You would come live here?>
<This is the most beautiful place in the world.>
97

<You have my permission to marry my daughter.>

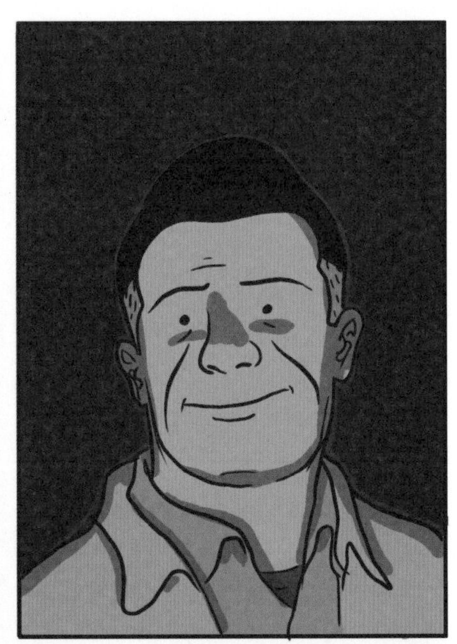

Dubai Bride

2218
2217

WE ARE TOGETHER. I LOVE YOU. I WANT YOU. WHY SHOULD I WAIT TO BE WITH YOU?
YOU ARE THE ONLY GOOD THING IN MY LIFE. I WON'T DISHONOR YOU. WE HAVE THE REST OF OUR LIVES TOGETHER.
IT'S JUST A LITTLE LONGER.

YOU ARE MORE TALIBAN THAN THE TALIBAN! WHEN THEY COME TO DUBAI THEY FUCK THEIR PROSTITUTES AND MISTRESSES.
"MORE TALIBAN THAN THE TALIBAN." I'LL PUT THAT QUOTE ON THE COVER OF MY NEXT BOOK!

MY GOAL WAS SIMPLE AND STRAIGHTFORWARD. I WANTED TO MARRY AFSANA AND LIVE PEACEFULLY IN SPLENDID ISOLATION.

THE PAKISTANI HALF OF KASHMIR PROVINCE WAS THE PERFECT RETIREMENT SPOT FOR A MAN RETIRED FROM A DANGEROUS PROFESSION. PAKISTAN USED TO CALL IT THE NORTHERN AREAS. NOW IT'S GILGIT-BALTISTAN.

IT WAS MORE THAN A LITTLE WILD WEST.

Gilgit, Gilgit-Baltistan region

THE PAKISTANI AUTHORITIES HAD VIRTUALLY NO PRESENCE. NO ARMY. NO POLICE. NO NEWS MEDIA. MOST OF THE LOCALS WERE OFFICIALLY STATELESS.
Ambush 250 m
point

UNLIKE THE TRIBAL AREAS BORDERING AFGHANISTAN LIKE WAZIRISTAN WHERE THE SKIES WERE FULL OF AMERICAN SPY DRONES LOADED WITH HELLFIRE MISSILES, PAKISTANI KASHMIR WAS OFF THE RADAR. FOR WHATEVER REASON, THE CIA AND OTHER SPY AGENCIES JUST DIDN'T PAY ATTENTION TO IT.

IT WAS THE LAST PLACE ANYONE WOULD COME LOOKING FOR ME.

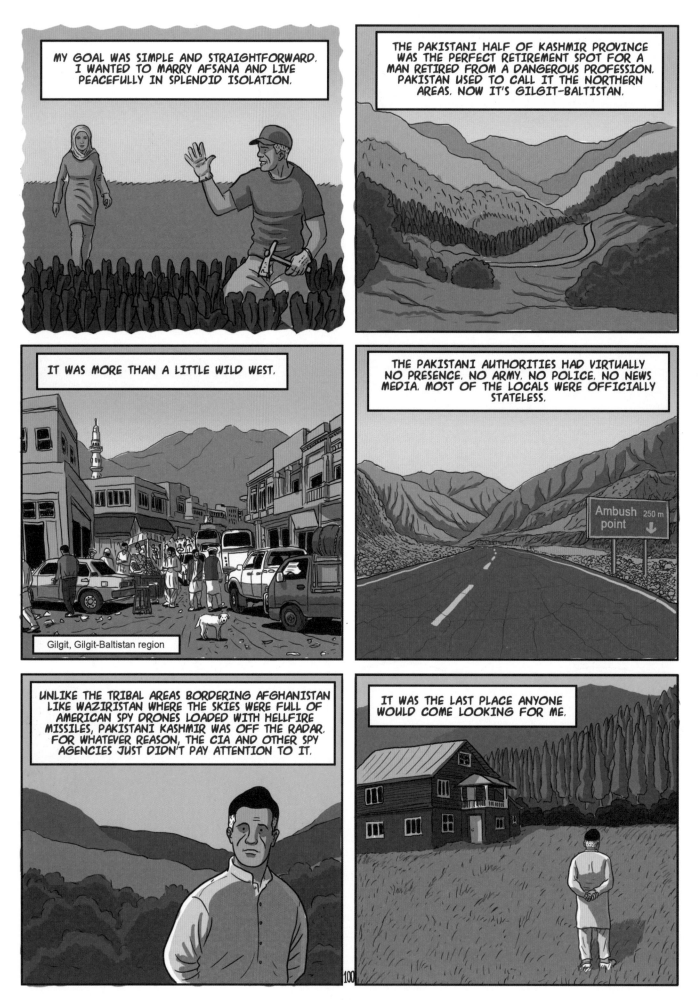

BUT IF THEY DID, THE TRIBAL CODE OF PASHTUNWALI WOULD ENSURE THAT I WOULD SEE THEM COMING WELL AHEAD OF TIME.
PLEASE TELL YOUR NEIGHBORS THAT I APPRECIATE THEIR MELMASTIA—HOSPITALITY—AND RESPECT.

AND THAT THERE MAY BE BAD MEN —OUTSIDERS— WHO BOTHER THEM ABOUT ME.

THESE GIFTS ARE TO COMPENSATE THEM FOR THEIR INCONVENIENCE IF AND WHEN THAT SHOULD OCCUR.

AND I WOULD BE READY.

101

Transit center, Manas International Airport, Bishkek, Kyrgyzstan (decommissioned)

TAP

Beep

Tian Shan Mountains, Kyrgyzstan

RROAARRRR

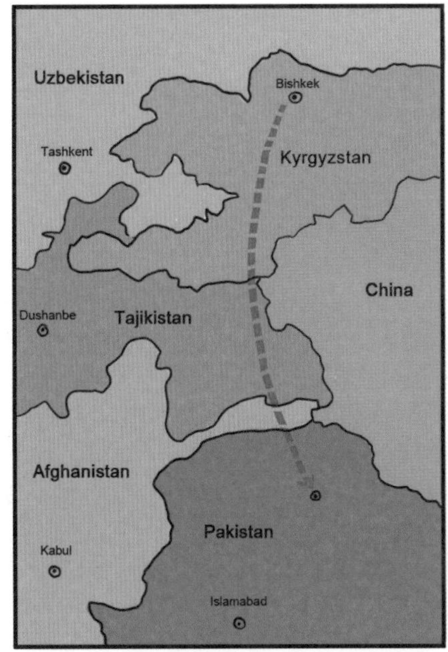
Uzbekistan
Bishkek
Tashkent
Kyrgyzstan
China
Dushanbe
Tajikistan
Afghanistan
Pakistan
Kabul
Islamabad

ЛЮБИТЕ СВОЮ РАБОТУ.
("LOVE YOUR WORK.")

ПОЖАЛУЙСТА, ВНЕСИТЕ ОСТАВШИЕСЯ 500 БИТКОЙНОВ В МОЮ УЧЕТНУЮ ЗАПИСЬ PAXFUL.
("PLEASE DEPOSIT THE REMAINING 500 BITCOINS INTO MY PAXFUL ACCOUNT.")

MARK SCRIBNER...
MY FAVORITE INTERNATIONAL JOURNALIST ARMS DEALER AND ALL-AROUND WARMONGER.
WHAT ARE YOU UP TO, REALLY?
3000 miles away, Agent Kuznetsov's office at the FSB in Moscow
103

I'M READY.

LUXUS GRAND
Lahore, Pakistan.

GOTTA LOVE THE IRONY. THE SECOND I GET OUT OF THE WAR-TROLLING BUSINESS...
HELLO?
DEPENDS WHO'S ASKING.

...I'M THE ONE WHO GETS ROLLED.
REALLY?

IN ONE IMPORTANT RESPECT VIRTUAL WARFARE IS EXACTLY LIKE THE OLD-FASHIONED BLOOD-AND-GUTS KIND.

IF YOU LET YOUR GUARD DOWN...
104

...YOU DIE.

MR. VICE PRESIDENT...?

I'LL CUT TO THE CHASE.

WE KNOW ABOUT YOUR NUKE.

IN YOUR CASE, MARK, A PICTURE IS WORTH *10,000* WORDS.
CLICK!

THAT, GENTLEMEN, IS AN SS-18 SATAN. EARLY 1980s, I BELIEVE. ONE OF SEVERAL THAT WENT MISSING AFTER THE COLLAPSE OF THE USSR.

LATE. PRETTY ARROGANT OF NATO TO RENAME ANOTHER COUNTRY'S WEAPON OF MASS DESTRUCTION.
THAT'S AN R-36M.

WHY, MARK? WHY DIDN'T YOU JUST TAKE THE WARHEAD? UNLESS YOU HAVE INFRASTRUCTURE WE'RE UNAWARE OF, ISN'T THE REST USELESS?
REDUCE, REUSE, RECYCLE. YOU NEVER KNOW WHEN SOMEONE MIGHT BE IN THE MARKET FOR AN ENGINE OR FUEL STORAGE TANK.

X MARKS THE SPOT.

YOU KNOW WHERE IT IS. YOU COULD DRONE THE FUCKER.
IF WE DIDN'T CARE ABOUT BLOWING UP A CITY WITH A QUARTER OF A MILLION PEOPLE.

WHAT WAS IT, TWO MILLION IN VIETNAM? A MILLION-PLUS IN IRAQ?
KAZAKHSTAN IS AN IMPORTANT U.S. STRATEGIC PARTNER IN CENTRAL ASIA.

WITH THE LARGEST UNTAPPED OIL RESERVES IN THE WORLD.
AS I SAID.
ANYWAY, IT'S USELESS WITHOUT THE DETONATOR MATERIALS.

AND HERE YOU ARE PICKING UP THE PETN AND HEXANITROSTILBENE.

DRONES. DON'T YOU EVER GET BORED NOW THAT VIOLATING BASIC PRIVACY RIGHTS IS SO EASY?
I CAN'T BELIEVE YOU THOUGHT YOU WERE GOING TO GET AWAY WITH THIS. YOU'RE GOING TO BE EXECUTED. EVEN THE EUROPEANS WILL APPROVE.

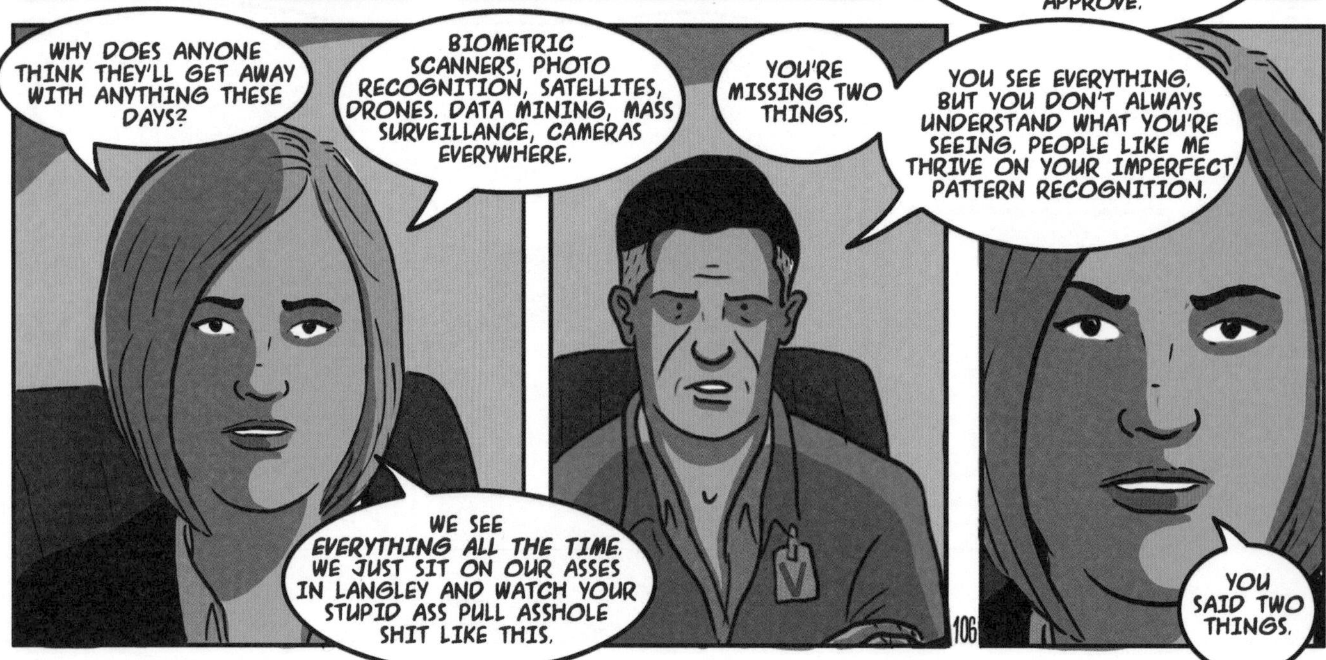
WHY DOES ANYONE THINK THEY'LL GET AWAY WITH ANYTHING THESE DAYS?
BIOMETRIC SCANNERS, PHOTO RECOGNITION, SATELLITES, DRONES, DATA MINING, MASS SURVEILLANCE, CAMERAS EVERYWHERE.
WE SEE EVERYTHING ALL THE TIME. WE JUST SIT ON OUR ASSES IN LANGLEY AND WATCH YOUR STUPID ASS PULL ASSHOLE SHIT LIKE THIS.
YOU'RE MISSING TWO THINGS.
YOU SEE EVERYTHING. BUT YOU DON'T ALWAYS UNDERSTAND WHAT YOU'RE SEEING. PEOPLE LIKE ME THRIVE ON YOUR IMPERFECT PATTERN RECOGNITION.
106
YOU SAID TWO THINGS.

TECHNOLOGY CUTS BOTH WAYS. ANYTHING YOU CAN USE, I CAN USE. YOU SEE ME, I SEE YOU.

CUT THE SHIT. IF YOU WERE GOING TO PROSECUTE ME WE WOULDN'T BE HAVING THIS CONVERSATION.
WHAT DO YOU WANT?

THE NUKE. AND THE DETONATORS. YOU WALK AWAY, WE'LL FORGET THE WHOLE THING.

A DEAL I CAN'T REFUSE.
EVER THE WORDSMITH.
DONE.

ONE MORE THING.
WHAT?

THE MONEY.
ALL OF IT.
YOU'RE NOT KEEPING YOUR BLOOD MONEY.
WHAT'S UP? NEED A SLUSH FUND FOR SOME COVERT OPERATION? "IRAN-CONTRA 2.0"?
107

YOU'LL WIRE TRANSFER EVERY LAST CENTIME TO THIS ACCOUNT. DON'T FUCK WITH US. WE KNOW ABOUT ALL YOUR ACCOUNTS. SEND ALL OF IT.
I WAS GOING TO SAY WE'RE SO ALIKE, BUT NOT REALLY.
I'M A BAD PERSON. EVIL, ARGUABLY.
BUT YOU—YOU'RE EVEN WORSE.

CLAP

CNN HQ
Text message
CNN HQ:
Call ASAP

MY BOSS NEVER SAW THE FUTURE UNTIL IT BIT HIM IN HIS FAT ASS, BUT HE WAS RIGHT THIS TIME. I HAD BEEN BLACKBALLED WITH THE IMPRESSIVE EFFICIENCY OF A NATION-STATE.

WHAT HAS SCRIBNER DONE TO OFFEND YOU?

QUESTION-ASKING TIME IS OVER. DOES YOUR NETWORK WANT ACCESS TO THIS ADMINISTRATION OR DOESN'T IT?

White House press secretary Sarah Huckabee Sanders

109

BRAAM

NOT MY PROBLEM.

PRESS
ID NUMBER: AT183321
ATLANTA OFFICE
MARK SCRIBNER
REPORTER
CNN
IMPACT YO
ORLD

110

IT WAS SO WEIRD: I DIDN'T CARE.

WAS I IN SHOCK?
OR JUST A SOCIOPATH?

SO WE'RE TRANSFERRING YOUR ENTIRE BALANCE, €182,100,906.95, TO THE ACCOUNT AT U.S. FEDERAL BANK OF NEW YORK FOR THE BENEFIT OF THE GENERAL FUND?

THAT'S CORRECT.

THE TRUTH IS —*THERE'S* A WORD!— I HAD EVERYTHING I WANTED.

THAT, I WAS ABSOLUTELY DETERMINED NOT TO MESS UP.
NOT BEFORE WE'RE TOGETHER.
WE *ARE* TOGETHER.

WE WILL ALWAYS BE TOGETHER. I WANT TO FEEL YOU.
I KNOW. ME TOO.

SOON.
111

THE NEXT MORNING.

I'M GOING TO THE GYM, SEE YOU LATER!

2105
2106

9:09 am
72%
Jason Levine, Atty
Feds confirm receipt of funds and ICBM.
They'll be in court Monday to drop charges.
I've asked them to execute an immunity guarantee.
You're clear now but remember—you've sworn, no more weapons sales.

112

HOW MANY FRIENDS DID YOU LOSE? HOW MANY FAMILY MEMBERS DID *I* LOSE?

YOU BETRAYED ME.

YOU BETRAYED THE IDEA OF LOVE!

MY GOD, HOW COULD YOU ACT LIKE—BECAUSE I KNOW YOU ARE NOT ACTUALLY—SUCH A MONSTER?

GOODBYE.

KABUL SERENA HOTEL

DANGER
MINES

AK-47
PAMIR CINEMA

AHMED ZAHIR, WE HARDLY KNEW YE. THE ELVIS OF AFGHANISTAN...

115

Hamid Karzai International Airport

KABUL INTERNATIONAL AIRPORT

LADIES AND GENTLEMEN, AS WE START OUR DESCENT TO ROMA-FIUMICINO AIRPORT, PLEASE MAKE SURE YOUR SEAT BACKS AND TRAY TABLES ARE IN THEIR FULL UPRIGHT POSITION, YOUR SEAT BELT IS SECURELY FASTENED AND...
THAT'S THE DIFFERENCE BETWEEN A LIVE REPORTER AND A DEAD ONE. OR A LIVE FORMER REPORTER.
ALWAYS GOTTA HAVE A PLAN B.
AND C, AND D...

HOW DUMB DID THE AMERICANS THINK I WAS? OF COURSE I HAD MULTIPLE ACCOUNTS.
GIOVANELLI
Banca privata
Roma
...AND HERE YOU GO, SIGNORE SCRIBNER.

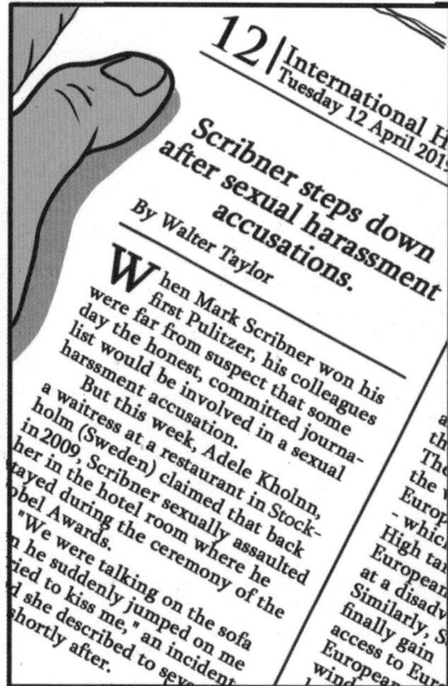
12
Tuesday 12 April
Scribner steps down after sexual harassment accusations.
By Walter Taylor
When Mark Scribner won his first Pulitzer, his colleagues were far from suspect that some day the honest, committed journalist would be involved in a sexual harssment accusation.
But this week, Adele Kholnn, a waitress at a restaurant in Stockholm (Sweden) claimed that back in 2009, Scribner sexually assaulted her in the hotel room where he
"We were talking on the sofa

"FAKE NEWS."

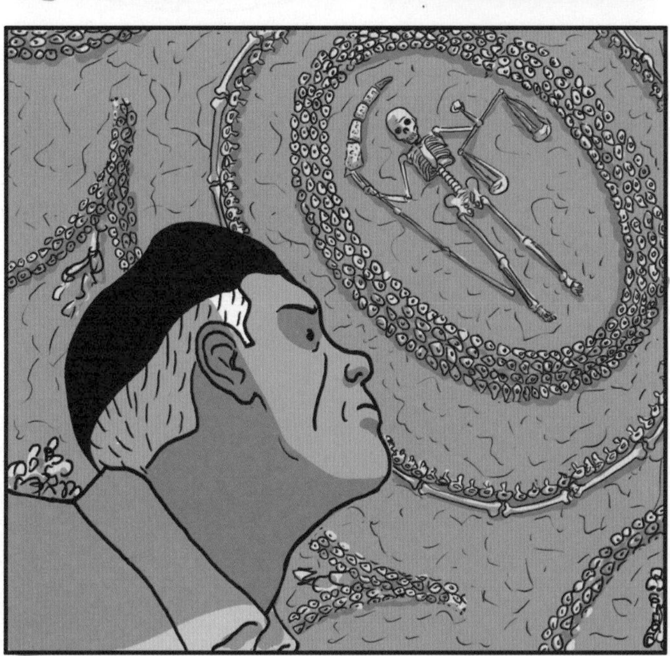

AGLIATELLA
Ristorante La Tagliatella

MENU
117

HEY MOM.
OH GOD, MOM, I'M SORRY.
I'M IN ROME. I'M GOING STRAIGHT TO THE AIRPORT.
I'M ON MY WAY.

PARTENZE - DEPARTURES

Orario Time	Volo Flight	Destinazione Destination	Inbarco Gate	Note Remarks
13:10	SQ0889	SINGAPORE	D2	CANCELLED
13:20	AE334	LONDON	J34	CANCELLED
13:20	JAL075	HONG KONG	B12	CANCELLED
13:20	IB124	MADRID	B8	CANCELLED
13:20	RY6432	BERLIN	C21	CANCELLED
13:20	RY556	OSLO	B14	CANCELLED
13:20	KLM 443	ST. PETERSBURG	C10	CANCELLED
13:20	SWS112	KIEV	A8	CANCELLED
13:30	AA390	ATLANTA	J8	CANCELLED
13:20	AA411	CHICAGO	A6	CANCELLED

Orario Time	Volo Flight	Destinazione Destination	Inbarco Gate	Note Remarks
13:35	AF0164	MANILA	A22	CANCELLED
13:35	BA332	LOS ANGELES	B12	CANCELLED
13:40	QA122	SIDNEY	J2	CANCELLED
13:40	AA112	BOSTON	C22	CANCELLED
13:40	JAL655	OSAKA	J5	CANCELLED
13:45	RY789	BRUSSELS	C7	CANCELLED
13:45	IB776	BARCELONA	A12	CANCELLED
13:45	TAP214	LISBOA	B14	CANCELLED
13:50	AF445	MEXICO	C9	CANCELLED

ATTENTION! THE AIRPORT IS CLOSED. THERE IS AN EMERGENCY.
WHY?
WHAT'S GOING ON?
SHOULD WE STAY?

OVER HERE!

SHOCKWAVES FROM THE BLAST WERE FELT AS FAR AWAY AS KANDAHAR AND JALALABAD...

THIS JUST IN: THE US GEOLOGICAL SURVEY'S INITIAL ESTIMATE IS THAT THE RELEASE OF ENERGY WAS EQUIVALENT TO 8.6 ON THE RICHTER SCALE. WE ARE NOT ABLE TO REACH OUR CNN BUREAU IN KABUL.
BREAKING NEWS
LIVE
MAJOR EXPLOSION IN KABUL
CNN
INCIDENT OF UNKNOWN ORIGIN - ALL COMMUNICATION SYSTEMS DISABLED
10:33 AM ET
ROKE NEWS THAT DOZENS OF VETERANS HAD DIED WHILE AWAITING TREAT
NEWSROOM

AFGHANISTAN IS SEISMICALLY ACTIVE. BIG EARTHQUAKES ARE NOT UNCOMMON THERE. THOUGH INFORMATION IS JUST BEGINNING TO TRICKLE IN, THIS FEELS LIKE IT MAY BE SOMETHING ELSE, SOMETHING BIGGER. WE WILL KEEP YOU UP-TO-DATE.
BREAKING NEWS
MAJOR EXPLOSION IN KABUL
THE AIRPORT IS CLOSED. EVERYONE MUST LEAVE!

THE G-20 IS MEETING NEXT WEEK IN LOS ANGELES TO DISCUSS—
Afsana
calling mobile...

THANK YOU FOR CALLING ME. PLEASE LEAVE YOUR MESSAGE.
Afsana
calling mobile...
THANK YOU FOR CALLING ME. PLEASE LEAVE YOUR MESSAGE.

IF VERIFIED, THIS WOULD MARK THE FIRST DETONATION OF A NUCLEAR DEVICE AGAINST CIVILIANS SINCE NAGASAKI AT THE END OF WORLD WAR II.

LOSION REPORTED IN KABUL, MANY DEAD

HE G20 TO EVALUATE THE SITUATION - UNITED NATIONS URGES TO KEEP CALM UNTIL THE S

120

121

THREE DAYS LATER.
DUSHANBE INTERNATIONAL AIRPORT
Dushanbe, Tajikistan

JUST TO THE BORDER.
BUT THE RADIATION—

LET'S GO.

Pyanj River border crossing, Tajikistan/Afghanistan
UN
UN

MEDECINS SANS FRONTIERES

HAZ
MAT

* "The Company" is argot for the CIA in particular, the US intelligence community in general.

IT'S IN THE CUSTODY OF THE U.S. GOVERNMENT.
NO. IT DISINTEGRATED OVER KABUL THREE AFTERNOONS AGO.

BUT THE EMBASSY FOLKS—THE UNDERCOVERS—
SORRY, MARK. NO, THEY WEREN'T. WELL, THEY WERE—BUT THEY WERE OFF THE RESERVATION. A ROGUE CABAL OF DEEP-STATE CRAZIES. THEY CONNED YOU OUT OF THE WEAPON SO THEY COULD MAKE A DRAMATIC GESTURE. SO THE U.S. WOULD NEVER BRING HOME ITS TROOPS.

VICE PRESIDENT PENCE—

THAT WASN'T MIKE PENCE. THEY FALSIFIED THAT VIDEO.

AT THE SAME EXACT TIME "PENCE" WAS TELLING YOU TO WIRE TRANSFER TENS OF MILLIONS OF EUROS—TO AN ACCOUNT, BY THE WAY, SET UP AS AN IRAN-CONTRA-STYLE SLUSH FUND—THE REAL PENCE WAS DELIVERING A EULOGY WITH ANGELA MERKEL.
Lahore consulate
28 april 13h34
Berlin
28 april 10h34
AND YEAH, I'VE ADJUSTED FOR THE TIME DIFFERENCE.

THE FUCKERS BLEW UP NEARLY FIVE MILLION PEOPLE. JUST TO ELIMINATE WHATEVER TINY CHANCE THERE EVER WAS THAT THE U.S. WOULD RAMP DOWN FROM ITS PERPETUAL WARFARE FOOTING AND PIVOT TO DOMESTIC SPENDING PRIORITIES THAT WOULD ACTUALLY HELP REAL PEOPLE.

19 YEARS IN AFGHANISTAN... 17 IN IRAQ...
IT'S NEVER ENOUGH FOR THEM. IT CAN NEVER EVER STOP.

124

GLOBAL MILITARY SPENDING IS $8 TRILLION A YEAR. THE U.S. IS 40% OF THAT. MORE THAN THE NEXT EIGHT COMBINED.

THEY CAN'T IMAGINE PEACE.
WHAT WOULD A WORLD WITHOUT WEAPONS LOOK LIKE? THEY DON'T WANT TO FIND OUT.
MEDECINS SANS FRONTIERES
MEDECINS SANS FRONTIERES

ALL THOSE PEOPLE DEAD.
BECAUSE OF ME.

DON'T BLAME YOURSELF. YOU WERE MERELY THE SUCKER.
IF THEY HADN'T FOUND YOU IT WOULD'VE BEEN SOMEONE ELSE.

YOUR NUKE WAS ATTRACTIVE DUE TO ITS LACK OF PROVENANCE AND THE FACT THAT POST-DETONATION FORENSICS WOULD POINT TO A NON-U.S. ACTOR.
PLAUSIBLE DENIABILITY.

I'M AN IDIOT. I TOOK THEM AT THEIR WORD.
VROOOM
VROOOM
JOURNALISM IS DEAD. BUT FACT-CHECKING STILL MATTERS.
125

BORDER IS OPEN.
VROOOM
VROOOM
YEAH... BYE, JAMES.

Afsana
calling mobile...
THANK YOU FOR CALLING ME. PLEASE LEAVE YOUR MESSAGE.
MEDECINS SANS FRONTIERES

SINCE KABUL AIRPORT WAS NO MORE, THE ONLY WAY INTO AFGHANISTAN WAS THE OLD TRANSIT ROUTE CROSSING THE PYANJ RIVER FROM TAJIKISTAN, THEN TRAVELING 250 MILES TOWARD THE BLAST RADIUS.
TAXI
TOYOTA
Kunduz-Taliqan Road
Taliban-controlled Northern Afghanistan

FASTER!
I KNOW!

OK, HOLD ON, HOLD ON...

LISTEN, YOU DON'T HAVE TO—

CRACK!

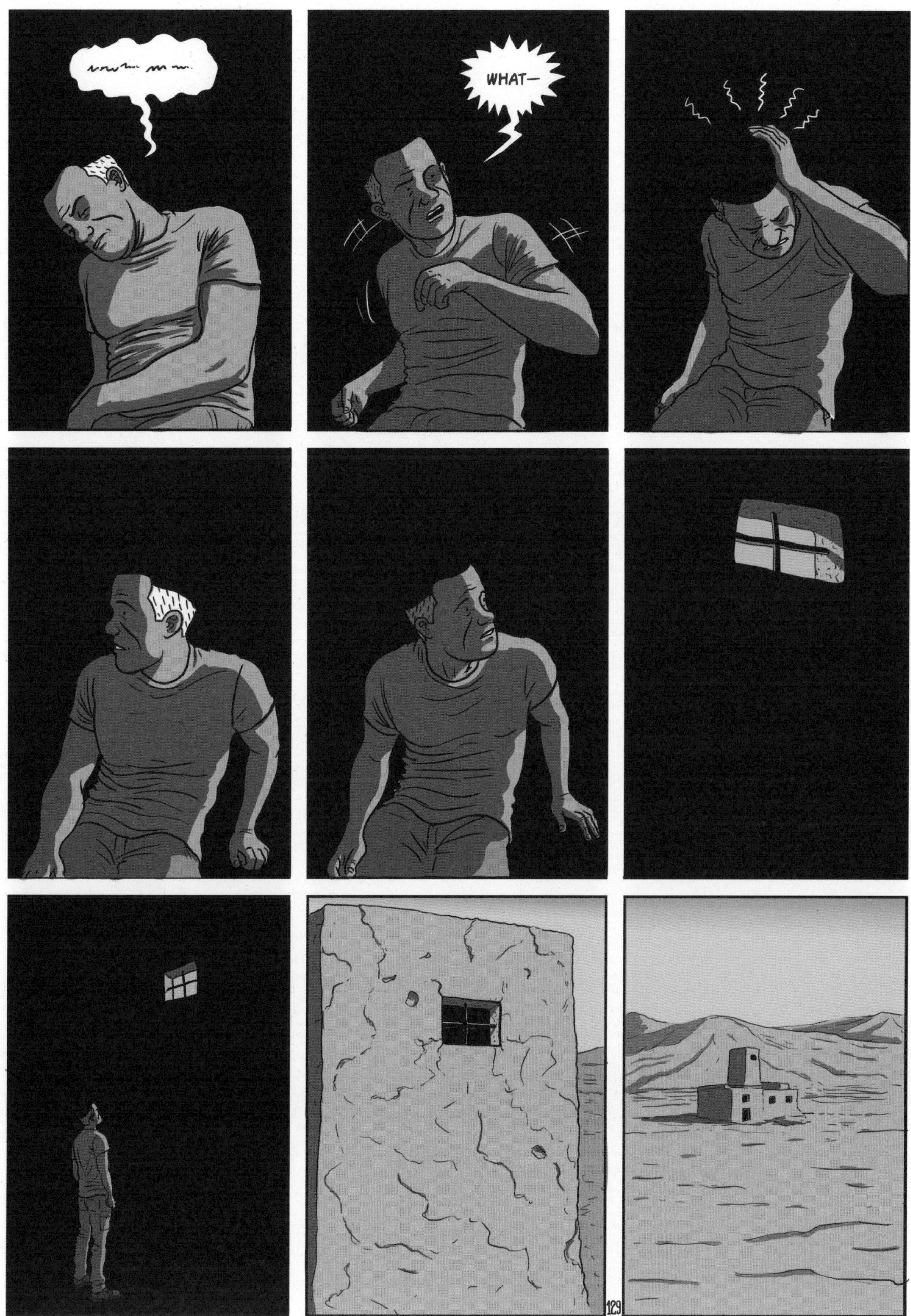
WHAT—
129

V

Afsana
Afsana
CLANC
CLANC
SCREEEECH
132

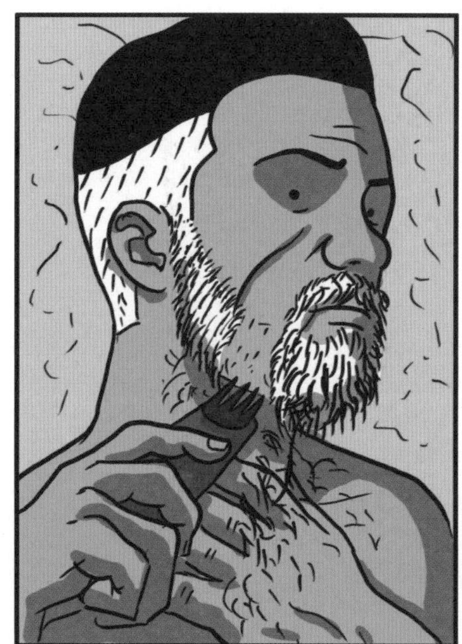

ALLAH IS KIND AND MERCIFUL. HE IS GIVING YOU BACK YOUR TELEVISION CAREER! YOUR RATINGS WILL HIT A CAREER HIGH!
THANK YOU.

I'D FEEL BETTER IF YOU WERE WEARING A MASK. IT WOULD MEAN YOU MIGHT NOT KILL ME, THAT I MIGHT BE RELEASED AND THAT YOU WOULDN'T WANT ME TO BE ABLE TO DESCRIBE YOU WHEN I WAS DEBRIEFED.

THIS IS NOT CNN. WE ARE NOT LIARS.

AHEM...

JOURNALISM CAN SAVE THE WORLD.
IT'S THE ONLY THING THAT CAN.
134

American

MARK SCRIBNER MAKES SOME STARTLING ALLEGATIONS, INCLUDING THAT ROGUE ELEMENTS WITHIN THE U.S. GOVERNMENT WERE BEHIND THE HORRIFYING NUCLEAR ATTACK IN AFGHANISTAN.

ISIS TORTURES ITS HOSTAGES. HE OBVIOUSLY ISN'T SPEAKING FREELY.
Washington
7:14 AM ET
ISIS HOSTAGE VIDEO
US: "WE DO NOT NEGOTIATE WITH TERRORISTS"
Becky Thompson | Deputy Secretary of State
CNN
6:14 AM PT

"FAHIM HAD A POINT. BUT NOT THE POINT HE THOUGHT HE HAD."

"VIRTUAL WARFARE IS LIKE THE OLD-FASHIONED KIND."

"THEY CAN'T IMAGINE PEACE."

"PLAUSIBLE DENIABILITY."

WHO CAN BELIEVE HIM?
Washing
7:14 AI
VITH TERRORISTS"
retary of State
6:14 AM

136

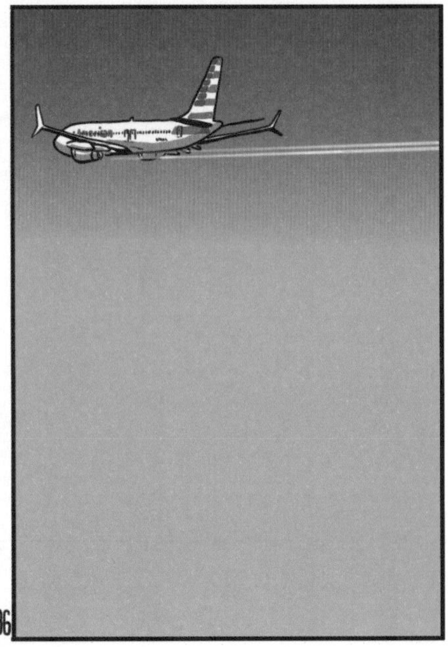

137

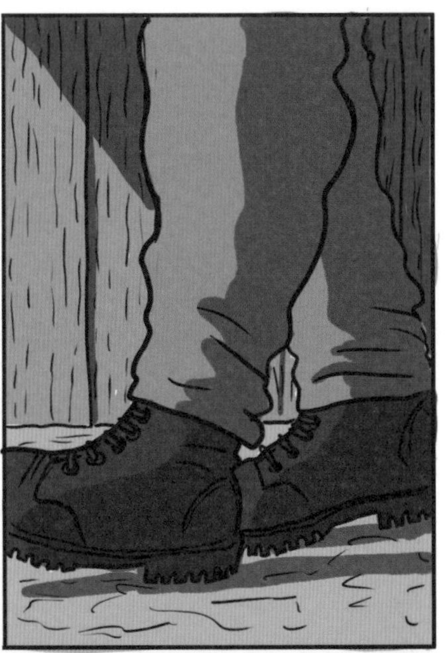

138

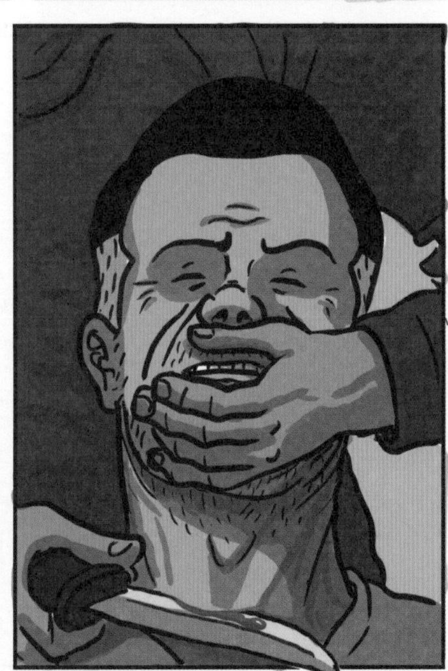

139

POWELL'S BOOKS
USED & NEW BOOKS
POWELL'S BOOKS
USED & NEW BOOKS
TED RALL
MARCH 23

80% OFF!
Mark Scribner
ASSIGNMENT NAMIBIA
Secrets and lies of war journalism
Unembedded in Iraq
Mark Scribner
Mark Scribner
Dispatches from Afghanistan
The New Media PARADOX
Mark Scribner

NY MOVING
FRAGILE
THIS SIDE UP

AGILE
SIDE U
2018 PULITZER PRIZE
International Reporting
MARK SCRIBNER

140

CRAAASH!

Make Love,
Not War

OFFICE SPACE FOR RENT
555-114-3000
WILL BUILD TO SUIT
555-114-3000
141

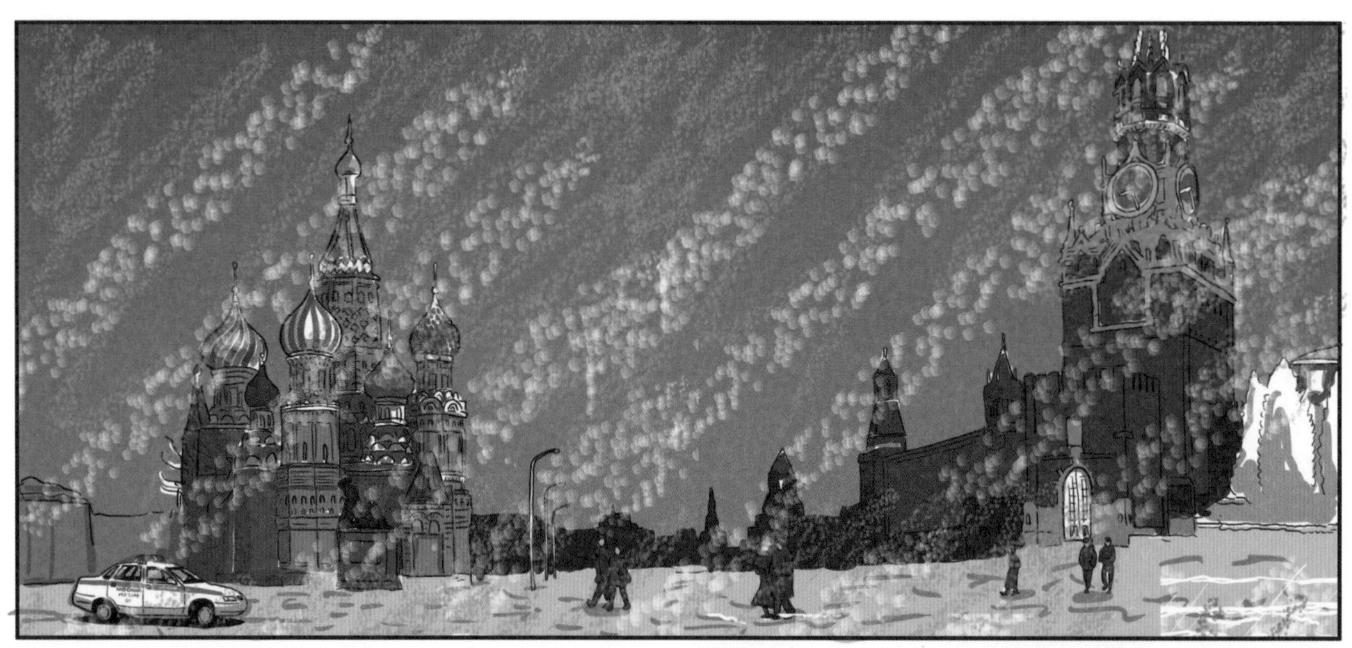

СТАНЦИЯ
ЛУБЯНКА

Federal Security Service of the Russian Federation, Lubyanka Building

buzzzzz

WE'RE ALL JUST BLUNDERING AROUND, BULLSHITTING OUR WAY THROUGH LIFE.
Status: EXECUTED BY ISIS

МИСТЕР СКРИБНЕР, ТЫ УМНЫЙ ДЬЯВОЛ! *
* (MR. SCRIBNER, YOU CLEVER DEVIL!)

DEEP FAKE.

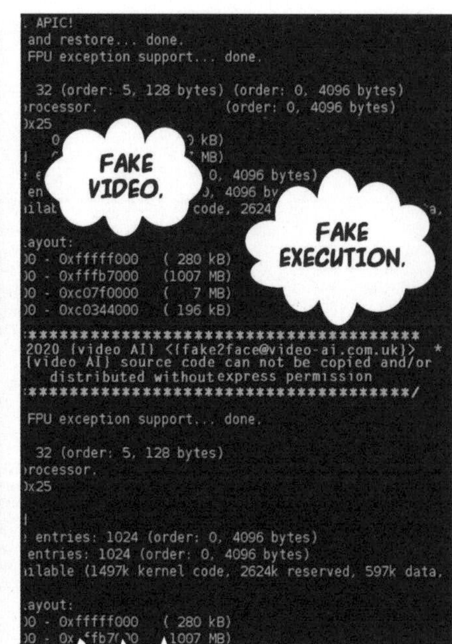
FAKE VIDEO.
FAKE EXECUTION.

MR. DIRECTOR?
UM...
WHAT'S UP?

WHAT? I'M BUSY WITH CHECHEN SHIT!
РОССИЯ

. . .

UH, CAN I HAVE TOMORROW OFF?

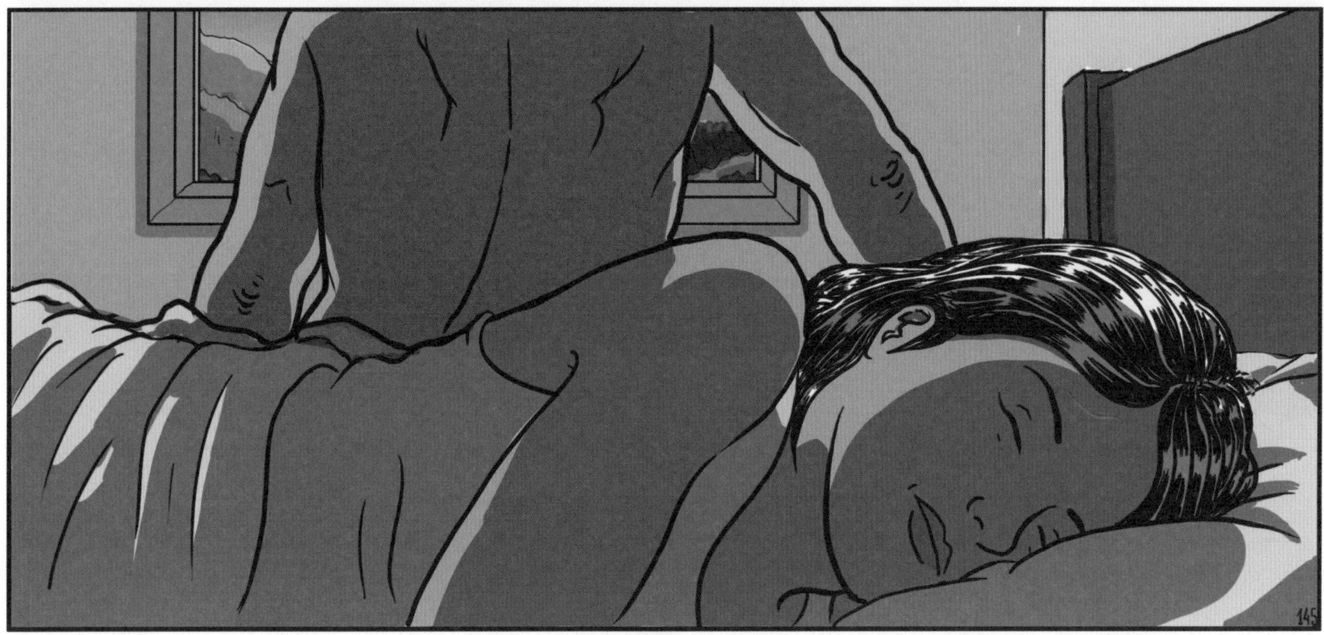
145

146

CHAI?
147

Also Available by Ted Rall from NBM:

The Year of Loving Dangerously

Rall's sympathetic account of his life on the edge encourages identifying with a situation so desperate that his outrageous choices seem necessary."
-Booklist

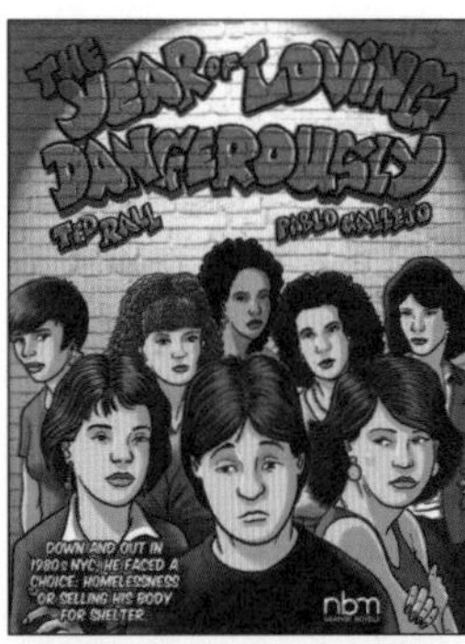

2024

"A rich, extremely clever and in many ways profound satire of where our "whatever" culture is taking us."
-Bradford W. Wright (author "Comic Book Nation"), Washington Post

To Afghanistan and Back

"For alternative views of post-9/11 politics, don't pass up this small, potent volume."
-Booklist

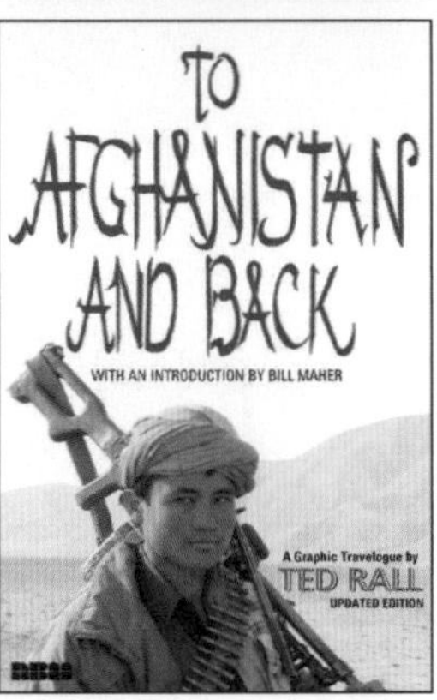

Silk Road to Ruin

"A rollicking, subversive and satirical portrait of the region that is part travelogue, part graphic novel. It's fresh and edgy and neatly captures the reality of travel in the region."
-Lonely Planet Guide for Central Asia

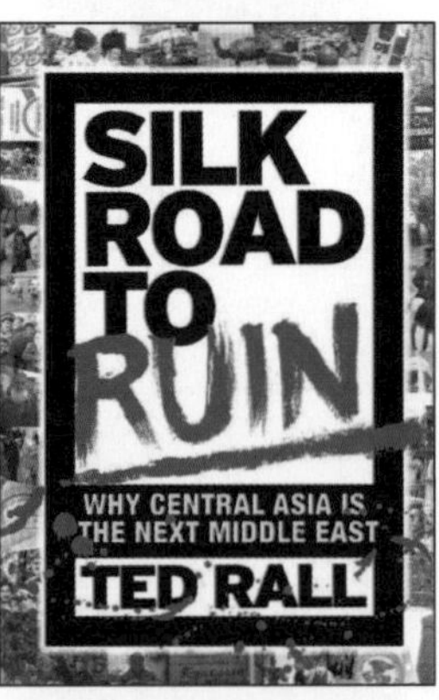

Ted Rall Online: www.RALL.com

Also available by Pablo Callejo from NBM:
with Rob Vollmar:
Bluesman
"In its knowing play of dark words and raw images, Rob Vollmar and Pablo Callejo's earthy graphic novel tells a tale worth hearing – and seeing. Bluesman, in the end, is a cathartic ghost story. Is there a better description of the blues?" - NPR

See previews, get exclusives and order from:
NBMPUB.COM
We have hundreds of graphic novels available.
Subscribe to our monthly newsletter
Follow us on Facebook & Instagram (nbmgraphicnovels), Twitter (@nbmpub).

NBM
160 Broadway, Suite 700, East Wing
New York, NY 10038
Catalog upon request